Snow, Stars and Wild Honey

by George P. Morrill

974.304
M

PINNACLE BOOKS   NEW YORK CITY

SNOW, STARS AND WILD HONEY

Copyright © 1975 by George P. Morrill

A Pinnacle Books edition, published by special arrangement with J. B. Lippincott Company

ISBN: 0-523-40-036-X

First printing, May 1977

Cover illustration by Oni

Photo insert courtesy of the author.

Printed in the United States of America

PINNACLE BOOKS, INC.
275 Madison Avenue
New York, N.Y. 10016

"... HEART-WARMING ..."
—Columbus *Dispatch*

"*In a text as consistently poetic as the lovely title—Morrill holds the reader enthralled ...*"
—*Publishers Weekly*

"**Written with a modest grace and good sense that somehow suit the subject the way butter suits bread.**"
—*Kirkus Reviews*

"Morrill is a beautiful writer, sensitive to the land and precise and elegant in his descriptions."
—*The Atlanta Constitution*

"**The narrative flows smoothly and easily, like a long letter from a friend, or a story told over a cup of coffee by a fire.**"
—*American-Statesman*

"*... Morrill writes with both humor and insight.*"
—*Library Journal*

"**... for everyone who has had an urge to get back to nature or seek a simpler lifestyle.**"
—Chattanooga *News-Free Press*

"... vividly recalls hardship and beauty ... Morrill made it—in the wild world and in the often wilder world of words."
—St. Louis *Post Dispatch*

For Phyllis and her sons

Contents

Snow, Stars and Wild Honey

A Personal Chunk . . .

WE HAD ALWAYS wanted a homestead in the wilderness.

During World War II, as a merchant seaman in far ports, I would get letters from my girl, Phyllis, saying that we ought to try a different pattern of life. Go pioneering in the backwoods. Build something out of the ordinary—like a birch-bark tepee or a mountain ranch.

I would draw a cabin plan and mail it back. I would visualize her—slim, blue-eyed, taffy-haired—examining it as she stood in the cluttered factory at Deep River, Connecticut, where she worked on Army gliders.

As months went by, it dawned on me that this mild-voiced girl in faded dungarees was even more determined than I was to latch onto some isolated territory of our own. Like me, she yearned for a personal chunk of America.

But after peace, money was short. Newly married, we lived with relatives. Wintered in a friend's summer bungalow. Camped in tents. We were grateful for

1

everyone's help; but, like other young people coughed up by the war, we were impatient of older generations—of their set ways and well-intentioned advice.

Then a baby, Pete, arrived in 1947. Our dream receded even farther into the background.

By that time I was earning our meager bread as a teacher in a makeshift veterans college in New London, Connecticut. "My fate," I said, "is to teach English to bored students at low pay—forever."

"Take our bankbook and head north," said Phyllis. "See what you can buy, and come rescue us."

I found a half-built cabin, tucked high on a mountain road near Saxtons River, Vermont. Brown with creosote and ringed with white birches, it looked out on an emerald May-world like a saucy toad—and the price was only $3,000.

Humphrey Neill, a bald, peppery Vermonter who lived in Saxtons River in a big yellow house set on soapstone blocks from a family quarry, agreed to take $1,000 down (our total fortune) and $37.75 a month for five years.

"If you try to winter up there, you're crazy," he said.

"We just want a summer camp."

Triumphantly bearing our mortgage deed, we sorted out our possessions in Connecticut. Some old lumber, one desk, a broken sled—cast-off stuff. I built a trailer out of some Ford rear wheels and boards from a chicken coop. We nailed together a cage for our mother cat and six kittens and tucked it into the trailer.

Stupid move—those cats? Well, they were special. The mother had come to us as a stray, round with young. Blackbeard himself could not have kicked her out. The kittens appeared, tumbly and independent, and we named them after people we admired:

2

Eleanor Roosevelt, Cordell Hull, Harry Truman, Wendell Willkie, Marian Anderson. We called the sassiest one Franklin D. Roosevelt.

On the way to Vermont the trailer blew a tire. I jacked her up and left Phyllis and Pete to guard while I took the wheel to a filling station and haggled over a tire. A sweating, red-faced mechanic sold me a used Goodyear for four dollars.

"If we make the state line, we've won," I said.

Phyllis grinned. "That's a definite maybe right now."

The last mile our fourteen-year-old Buick strained and blew steam. The cats threw up and worse—and at first we mistook their stench for the aroma of fertilized fields. But we came out on acres bathed in sunlight, and the faint *shssssssssss* of waving timothy flowed through us like a prayer.

"We're home," said Phyllis.

The place was officially titled Hartley Hill, although everyone called it a mountain. At 1,490 feet, it hulked taller than Snake Mountain near Vergennes or Granville Notch north of the Snow Bowl. But from the start, its massiveness was gentle on our hearts.

The cabin wasn't really all that much. But Phyllis floated through it, exclaiming, touching the knotty-pine cabinets.

"The floor is *even*," she cried, stamping her foot.

The place consisted of two 15 by 15 foot rooms, a kitchen, and—unbelievably—a bathroom fed by a gravity-flow spring. It had yard-square windows that opened inward from the top. Its naked two-by-fours gave off a clean, piny smell. Two stoves—one of sheet metal and the other an ancient cast-iron model with a small oven—dominated each section.

The eastern room even boasted a low-raftered attic, reached by creaky stairs. That gave us storage space, and a place to read in solitude on an old mattress. The whole cabin looked small from the outside; but, with its nook beneath the stairs, its big closet in the west room, and its crannies under the eaves, it fooled you. There were a lot of places for pack rats like us to stow our ridiculous little treasures; and we would soon have the place overflowing with paperbacks, lifting weights, clothes baskets, and Tonka toys.

Rough, unfinished, this interior still glowed, honey-soft, when the sun reached in. And there wasn't a single leak stain along the ceiling.

I took Phyllis outside and got her to tap her fist on our solid hemlock siding. The cabin rested on concrete piles, some made by pouring concrete into open-ended nail kegs. Since the site was slanting, partly on ledge, we could scrunch under the western end of the structure and see the old barn beams, junk two-by-sixes, and rough slabs that held the place up. The eastern end vanished in the hillside (we were too green to realize that this part of the foundation would rot and would have to be rebuilt in a few years).

"We have a palace here, Zeke," she said, twanging the words.

"No flies on us'n, Marthy."

It didn't matter a bit that we had to sleep on the floor.

The back door opened onto a huge poplar tree, whose roots had partly lifted the wooden stoop. On every side birches, white as marble, arched over the roof. Our little house was a growth of the forest—as natural to the ferny floor as a mushroom.

We made our beds under the windows of the east room. We set Pete's crib near the door so we could throw him out in case of fire. Two years old, he was

4

rugged and scrambly, and I secretly suspected that in an emergency *he'd* be the one to sound the alarm and save the plantation.

Phyllis cooked our first breakfast on an outside grate.

Suddenly a voice shouted, "Hey!" Under the birches stood a short, wrinkle-faced old man in a denim cap. He waved a thorn cane at us. "I'm Richard Bradley, from the farm down yonder."

He looked us over with bright, wind-bitten eyes. Fingering the cane in his knotty fist, he offered the hope that we would take to the mountain and it would take to us.

"We're blessed with good things up here—fresh air, plenty water—like a that," he said. "I wouldn't live downtown if you give me six bred heifers and a new hay wagon."

He hardly looked like a farmer. He wore a clean white shirt and a black bow tie. Only months later, after we had marked him as a valued friend, did we realize that he always dressed this way for Sunday, which day it was.

"Some things for you at the farm. Stop by," he said. "Eggs, greens—like a that."

He said, "No, thanks," for coffee. He lifted his cane and left with a bumpy gait.

Throughout the next long, dreamy weeks we explored our property, luxuriating in the *feel* of ownership. Pete ran squealing after butterflies. He made other acquaintances too. He found a fat jade frog in the brook. He saw a porcupine bristle across the field—and pointed in amazement when a strange dog ran by, yipping, its muzzle full of quills. He cried over a field mouse, killed by Franklin D.

Above the cabin stretched a level area that we quickly named the Flat. Beyond it a tangle of black-

5

berry bushes, weeds, and a dead elm surrounded the remains of a small pond. The pond's dam had fallen through; its shards of concrete and stone littered the brook. I puzzled over how such a peaceful trickle of water could dislodge so bulky a weight. My acquaintance with the mountain's wild water was yet to come.

Across our bridge (a creaky collection of wagon planks and barn beams) a two-rut road curved through the clover. It passed a wind-twisted apple tree and led to our prize spot: the Knoll.

The Knoll was the property's glory. It mounded up like a jelled tidal wave, mottled with shades of green—cobalt, avocado, lime. Queen Anne's lace, black-eyed Susans, wild strawberries—these and other hit-or-miss vegetation sprouted there. From the Knoll we looked out on the heaving sea of the Green Mountains to the west. To the northeast, far across the Connecticut River, a peak in New Hampshire shone in the sun. Nearer, two miles down, twin steeples jutted from Saxtons River—toys in ivory.

A barn had once stood on the Knoll, facing the hammer of the north. Decades of storm and heat-blast had wrecked it. The only solid remains were a few foundation rocks. But it had scattered a legacy, a precious thing—rich soil. Long ago, generations of cattle had left deposits of manure and urine. Everything that the farmer's shovel and spreader missed had seeped into the earth. The result was a crop of strong hay, green as berylline and packed with nutrient, sticking up where long-vanished dairymen had once worked at milk stools.

The Knoll beckoned at all hours. In the morning the sun didn't rise above the eastern slope until around nine o'clock, so dew webs shimmered on the grass while the valley below baked in lemony heat.

We could walk barefoot, cooling our toes in fragrant wetness.

By noon the Knoll blazed. We could stretch out on an old Army blanket, tanning and baking, while merciful breezes laved our backs.

At sundown, the clouds put on ponderous displays, miles long and high—tumbling slowly, turning red, then purple. We could sit on the Knoll, chewing grass, and make out monster sky-figures—knights, ships, elephants—marching toward Boston.

And at night—ah. On the Knoll we became half-inch hop-o'-my-thumbs in a black-velvet Tiffany tray, ringed with brilliance. Stars seemed to teeter on our eyelids. An owl hooted. A fox barked. The universe was good, and we knew we had a rightful place in it.

Back from the Knoll, the ground dipped. And, surprisingly for this elevation, a swamp glistened, full of rank growth. Here was the home of purple dragonflies, hard-backed beetles, and other weird insect life. Sloshing through the mud, we had the nervous feeling that some mythical serpent with a mean, Nile-green head might rise up, dripping.

South of the swamp, the land tilted upward. Crowded with trees—evergreens, maples, oaks—it was a sanctuary of moss and coolness, a cathedral place to meditate in. Sunlight chinked it with yellow; and viewed from the Knoll in autumn, it became a many-colored tapestry. It bordered a dirt road on the east, which led farther up the mountain. Across the road loomed Big Baldy and Little Baldy, granite outcroppings that belonged to Bradley but that we were to hike and learn to love.

This was our turf, "containing [so the deed said] 6¾ acres of land be the same more or less surveyed by George F. Webb during July of 1946. . . ." The deed bore two carmine U.S. documentary stamps, engraved

7

with likenesses of L. Woodbury and Wm. H. Crawford (whoever they were). They made the whole layout officially ours.

So the summer passed. Leaving for the winter, we grew pensive. As I nailed the windows shut, I felt strange, like a troop commander abandoning an outpost.

"So long, Vermont."

Washing dishes again in our rented Connecticut place, Phyllis couldn't get the mountain out of her mind. Suddenly she said, "Why can't a family dig in up there? You'd never need a business suit. I'd never need French heels."

An all-season place to try our sinew in? A place to collide with the elements and see if we could win?

"Wal-l—," I said.

We hashed it out, and our assets (aside from specie) looked better and better. Phyllis was a part-Swede village girl whose forebears were down-to-earth farmers. She could cook, run a trim house, and proffer a saw or hammer at the right moment. Besides, she had a schoolteacher's degree, which might come in handy.

Best of all, she liked to laugh—and she wasn't afraid of much.

I had grown up in her small town. I, too, owned a degree from a small university (Wesleyan). And, in addition to sailoring, I had worked as a road laborer, a pipe coverer, and a longshoreman on the Bermuda docks.

"If we hang around here," I said, "this is the scenario—rat-race job, little house with big mortgage...."

"Dull parties."

"Clothes and cars—"

"—with fat time payments."

"Lawn-mowers."

8

"In-laws."

By mid-February we had talked ourselves into it.

"We'll just cut loose and go up there, like Sherman's army," I said. "No supply lines."

Phyllis had smacked her dishrag into the sink. "Zeke the Mountain Man has spoken."

Too-Early Expedition

APRIL, 1949. On a slate-colored Thursday afternoon I gunned the old Buick up to Saxtons River again. I passed the Bradleys' sagging horse barn and a lumpy stone wall, and I lifted my hand in salute.

Greetings, homeland.

I was back alone on this crash weekend to buy tools, build partitions, construct bunk beds, and chop firewood. "Feather that nest for our permanent hop in June, Zeke," Phyllis had ordered.

All winter long in Connecticut we had dreamed sweet dreams of our lonely retreat. We had schemed and plotted and saved dimes in a jar. I carried enough money for three days' food and gasoline—and a down payment for tools. According to the phone book, there was a Sears store in Keene, New Hampshire, twenty-five miles from Hartley Hill, and I would do my buying there.

I rammed the Buick up a rise. The road narrowed, then petered out to yawning mud. The car shuddered, then halted, hub-deep. I lugged food, blankets, knapsack, and one wet copy of *The New York Times* half a mile uphill to the cabin.

Darkness fell, cooler than I had expected. I opened the spring, my numbed fingers straining with a valve under two feet of ice water. I lighted the Coleman lantern, cut some wood, built a stove fire, and spread my blankets.

After a supper of beans and coffee, I stepped outside. The spongy turf was starting to refreeze. I carried a couple of stones to prop up our wagon-wheel gate, which had slumped in winter storms. Four miles across the valley a dot-sized light twinkled—Cutts, our only visible neighbor.

Vermont, I think we'll hit it off. . . .

Trudging back to the cabin, I kicked silver tusks of icicles lying half-melted under the trees. It was certainly getting colder. As I crawled under my blankets, the squeaky, clumpy talk of naked birches began. Ah, romantic north wind.

I fell asleep, feeling the same sweet loneliness I used to enjoy far out at sea.

When I awoke, the fire was dead. I stood up, quaking with cold. Snow billowed past the windows, frothy as malted milk. I downed breakfast (two peaches). I waded through four inches of snow back to the car, started her, and got her rocking, but she wouldn't come free.

I slogged back to the cabin, brought a shovel to the car, and started digging under the wheels. Without warning, the shovel broke.

I flung the shovel away. I gunned the car back and forth. Suddenly—SNAP. The motor hummed but nothing happened.

Broken axle.

Richard Bradley was careful not to smile at the mud-caked, snow-dusted apparition in his doorway.

11

His wife gave me coffee while his hired man, Si Finch, harnessed up a team of horses. Si and I looped a chain around the bumper.

"Eyah!" Si yelled.

The horses lurched forward. *Ka-whang*. The bumper snapped.

An hour later we towed the car to the Bradleys' yard, safely chained around the axle. I walked two miles and borrowed a jeep from Humphrey Neill. *Come hell or hailstones, I will damn well get those tools in Keene*. The road was deep with slush and freezing rain, and I skidded around groaning sand trucks.

At Sears the clerks were pleasant, but they wouldn't sell me anything until they checked my credit in Connecticut. That couldn't be until tomorrow because their finance officer . . . etcetera, etcetera.

I picked out a stock in anticipation, anyhow—hammer, screwdriver, wrenches, square, screws, nails. Four heavy cartons, totaling over $150.

"I'll be back tomorrow to pick this up," I said.

When I took the jeep back to the Neills, they insisted that I stay for supper. Gratefully I stayed all night, taking a bath in the oldest tub in Saxtons River (zinc sheathing over a deep wooden frame).

In the morning Humphrey led in his jeep while I rolled the Buick down from the Bradleys'. Suddenly I heard a scraping noise. The wheel was rubbing the fender. I climbed down. The whole business—wheel and axle—was *coming out*. I jacked up the car and pushed them back, then resumed rolling. A moment later, *scrape-scrape*. For the next two hours we lifted the car and pushed back wheel and axle every 100 feet.

A quarter of a mile from O'Connor's Garage, the jack broke.

It was early afternoon before we limped into the

garage, with the aid of a borrowed jack. Bob O'Connor, an unruffled car fixer who had seen everything, said yep, he could get a new axle from Brattleboro—tomorrow, maybe. A quick call to Sears brought the first sunshine ray—my credit was all right. My cartons were waiting.

Ashamed to ask for Humphrey's jeep again, I negotiated a round-trip ride with a pickup heading for Keene. The farmer had to make stops for feed bags, eggs, bill payments, and half a dozen other matters. By the time we reached Sears the doors were closing, and it took impassioned pleas to get the last clerk to give me my cartons. The farmer helped me heave them aboard.

Back at Saxtons River, I stowed the heavy cartons at O'Connor's Garage. I stumbled the two miles up our pitch-black road, once sprawling flat in the ruts. Inside the cabin, I found that the only matches in my pocket were wet. I ate a can of cold soup and wrapped up in my blankets.

The next morning it rained. I wallowed through slop—half mud, half snow—to the garage. By noon the axle was repaired, and Bob O'Connor agreed to bill me the following month.

Victory at last? I gunned the car to the Bradleys', recklessly slamming through new mush-spots in the ruts. Beyond the farm the road was impassable, a mud lake. Richard lent me a heavy sled, and I transferred the big cartons to it, planning to tow it over what slushy snow was left.

As I tugged the sled out of the yard, my ear caught an odd sound: *Pssssssssssssssst.*

The right rear tire of the Buick was leaking. I peered at the sky. *Locusts next, Lord? The Black Death?* The Bradleys gave me some stove logs to jam under the axle. At last I took off.

It was a tough tow. Bending almost double, I

13

hauled the sled up a steep hayfield bordering the road. After every five fence posts I gave myself a rest. One-two-three-four-five—rest. The rhythm was exhausting, but I dared not break it. Once collapsed in the slush, I was sure I would fall into everlasting sleep.

After lunch beside a roaring stove (at the garage I had planted dry matches in all six pockets), I unloaded my treasures. Oo ... that gleaming hammer, that razor-toothed saw. Mmmm ... the oily scent of virgin wrenches.

Then I started searching the brown bags—frantically. *The clerk had left out the nails.*

I could at least measure and cut. I sawed some scrap lumber into pieces for the bunk beds and numbered them with a pencil. Around sundown, a splinter went under my thumbnail and broke off.

Then I discovered that the gas for the Coleman lantern was used up.

It was a memorable Vermont evening, picking at the splinter with a tack by the light of the stove and listening to mice. Before falling to sleep, I started to cough. ...

The next day I had to leave. First, chilled and shaking, I changed my flat tire. Then I said good-bye to the Bradleys and pressed the starter.

Nothing.

"Dead battery's no worse than a busted arm," said Richard. He and Si helped push the car to the road. After a thirty-foot roll, the motor kicked in.

Back in Connecticut, I restrained my epic of woe. Throttled my cough. Hid my inflamed hand. Then I rose from my mother-in-law's table and hit my shoulder against a shelf loaded with antique cups.

With a sickening *crash-tinkle*, the whole shelf tumbled down.

Battening Down the Hatches

WHEN JUNE CAME, we weren't really ready for our permanent jump. (The crash weekend in April had accomplished only a tenth of what I had planned.) But we packed the trailer anyhow and said good-bye to Connecticut.

"I'll find a job someplace," I said.

"We have food money until September," said Phyllis, who was five months pregnant. "That's something."

That was everything. It gave us time to think. We started the habit of turning problems around in our minds, squinting at them from all angles—not concentrating on what we couldn't do but on what seemed possible. Now take this squeaky-doored cabin, these raggle-taggle acres begging for hands. . . .

First, I nailed together the bunk beds.

Second, I partitioned the east room into three sections—two bedrooms and a miniscule library. Pete's room had a built-in bookcase, soon jammed with Little Golden Books. Phyllis's and mine boasted a knotty-pine closet with a clothes rack made out of a broomstick.

Third, I recovered a pile of stove-length hardwood under some leaves. Only part was rotten. I stacked it by the door and covered it with tar paper weighted by stones.

Fourth, we found that our tumbledown log fence lining the road was fastened to its sagging posts by 14-inch, ⅜-inch bolts.

"They're worth dough," I said.

"There's our reserve fund," said Phyllis.

With an adjustable wrench and pliers, we twisted off the rusty nuts, hammered the bolts back through the posts, and dumped them into coffee cans full of guts-oil from the Buick. We gleaned over 200 bolts.

"I can get a dime apiece for those—cash money," I said.

(As it happened, we never liquidated this hoard. But we knew it was there—a comforting backstop. Instead, we used the bolts in a dozen different money-saving ways. Year by year those handy steel rods, bent or straight, were to become foundation bolts for new construction, braces, repair cleats, handles, S-hooks to hold paint cans. . . .)

Next we eyed a 5-by-5-foot outhouse about forty feet from our back door. Sound and nicely shingled, it boasted an elaborate wooden vent through the roof.

"I guess the bathroom was a luxurious afterthought—thank heaven," said Phyllis. "Now that outhouse has got to go."

"I could make it into an office *if* we could move it," I said, "but we can't."

For years I had been writing stories and poems. I had tried a few on editors with no luck. Then suddenly a fiction piece about the South Pacific (where I had sailed during the war) had sold to *Colliers Weekly*—for the fabulous price of $750. Ever since, although nothing more had been accepted, I had demanded at least the semblance of an office to typewrite in.

"Why can't we move it?"

"It must weigh two thousand pounds," I said.

"Don't sailors move things with ropes?"

"Well—if they have a steam winch."

We both looked at our 1935 coupe. There was our energy source—150 horses under a blister-pocked hood. I bought some one-inch Manila and a pair of blocks. I rigged the tackle to a large tree and hooked onto the car, then lashed the rope end to the building. Phyllis drove the car slowly across the Flat while I ministered to the straining hawsers. The outhouse staggered up a small granite ledge, tearing blackberry bushes.

I crowbarred the building onto brick piles. I cut two windows in the walls and built in a small desk made of scrap planks. I even chopped a gap in the forest to give me a view of the valley. After two days' struggle, there stood the perfect writing shack—and I could only pray that the previous function of the structure wouldn't influence the type of material it would now produce.

Lesson One: A car is a power tool. Use it.

Thereafter, our confidence grew. There were limitless ways to improve our property at little or no cost—if we thought about them. Even the ridiculously obvious ones gave a sense of satisfaction. We hunted out flat rocks, dragged them behind the car, and built a walk to our front door. Pete hauled one brick at a time in his toy wagon and piled them for future projects. I cut down trees, laid them across the brook, packed them with sod, and dammed up a wading pond big enough for us to float in. After hours of primitive toil, we would lie there while the water chattered over us, watching Pete play with boats

17

made of shingles and leaves. We dubbed the spot Pete's Pool in his honor.

Lesson Two: Take time out from any work to enjoy your country pad. It's what you came out there for.

Summer storms arrived, great cracklers barreling down the valley. From the Knoll we watched huge snake tongues leap out of the clouds, dazzling white. Then a comber of wind would advance through the lower trees. As soon as the first puff hit our cheeks, we fled to the cabin. Anyone who has not experienced an electric storm on a lonely mountainside has missed one of nature's mightiest thrills.

The sky boomed, flashed, roared. The roof trembled. Occasionally we'd hear *c-crack-splinter* and know that some nearby treetop had caught a few million volts. Phyllis and Pete huddled on our bedding while I strutted about pretending unconcern. Rain pounded the eaves, a frightening Niagara that made the whole building shake.

After each storm we ventured out—and rediscovered a hard fact of country living: you are forever in keen conflict with the elements. Shattered limbs (mostly dead wood) littered the ground and roof. New runoffs gnawed at our foundation.

During one particularly violent storm the wind pushed a leaning rake through my writing-shack window and the water hammered a leak in our old-fashioned fiber car top. We cleared up the debris, noting that each gale could be expected to supply stove wood for at least two days. We filled in the gullies and dug shallow trenches to direct future storm water away from the house. I bought a twenty-nine-cent glass cutter and carved a pane for the writing shack from some big dusty pieces found in the attic. Finally, I dragged out the old Army tent and fashioned a semi-garage for the Buick.

We timed the entire repair operation at about seven hours. But then we added a couple of hours more upon discovery that a limb had jabbed a hole in some shingles. In all, a sobering experience. Out here nature dictated how a lot of our time would be spent.

Lesson Three: The easy country vacation you read about is based on work.

Other lessons kept coming. Vermont nights can be freezing in August. Honeybees sting like needles. You can slice off a good-sized hunk of thumb sharpening a scythe. . . .

We did everything we could think of to get ready for a brutal winter. We traded the old car for a secondhand jeep. We wrapped the foundation around with doubled-over construction paper. I built braces of green saplings between the concrete piles on the inside so that the wind would not burst the tender cellulose wall.

Along the outside we laid logs and evergreens. I built a lean-to in which to store excess stuff. I packed tent canvas around the bottom and secured it with stones.

Next, we caulked the window frames with strips of felt, some cut from old hats. I knew we ought to buy storm windows; but, since this was out of the question, we tacked sheets of plastic over the glass, leaving dead-air space between. At first the diffused images through these windows were annoying, but we got used to them. And at sunset the lollipop hues—the carmines, China blues, and ambers—made the place glow like a bargain-basement Fantasia.

We made two storm doors out of screen doors by covering them with heavy paper from grocery bags, waterproofing it with varnish, and nailing it down with thin kindling wood. The finished doors were really too heavy for their hinges, and one was to be shattered by wind. But they sealed in a lot of heat during the worst months.

We shoveled earth over the sills at the east end of the house where it butted into the embankment.

We added all the firewood we could chop to the pile by the door (a veritable mountain) and shielded it with tar paper.

We walked around the rooms to find where cold air trickled in. We plugged all the holes with putty.

As a precaution, Phyllis assembled and patched every bit of fabric we could find—old blankets, worn-out sweaters, coats, and throw rugs. Piles were placed in strategic places such as the attic, bedroom, and front closet, in case the roof leaked or a window blew in and our bedding got soaked. In one old trunk we even had a high-quality woolen Stars and Stripes, salvaged in 1946 from a merchant ship, awaiting emergency duty as a bunk coverlet.

"Now we need two things—a job and a bank loan," I said.

I began a work search. My credentials included navigating transworld tankers and correcting freshman themes—not much help. Humphrey Neill suggested trying a new small business, Readex Microprint, in Chester, thirteen miles away. Shortly, I was sitting opposite Albert Boni, president of Readex, at his old Colonial house on Chester's Main Street. I laid out my cards.

"Fifty dollars a week," he said.

I looked at Albert. He was a small, hawk-nosed man with a bush of gray-white hair. He had a crisp, bright way of speech that bespoke authority. Something about him promised fascinating days.

I explained that I needed sixty a week to make ends meet.

He shook his head.

I got up to go. "Well, thanks for your time."

"All right, sixty," he said. "But not until after thirty days when we see how things shape up."

So I became a printer, coaxing the jeep to Chester every day, leaving Phyllis and Pete to go on with winter preparations. I worked in an old wooden mortuary converted to a printshop.

Next I went after the bankers. They, however, were unenthusiastic. One lifted a brow at our unfinished rafters, at the wet socks hanging over a wood stove.

"Winter's just a whoop away," he said, edging out the door. "Move to town, young folks."

Phyllis only smiled. "But we're *invested* here."

The fourth moneyman I tried, an ash-haired Vermonter named Z Persons, listened to my raptures over our property. Say, we had space—a lordly view. At night, stars glowed like zircons. These September days were yellow-and-green music. He ought to come up and look at the sweetest acres in southern Vermont.

His steely eyes examined me. Then he said, "Sounds like a proposition for chipmunks and summer dudes."

He lent us $500.

What first? We decided on a fireplace and a power system. I bought a shovel and started digging the foundation for the fireplace. Phyllis sent to Sears-Roebuck for a book entitled *Electric Wiring: How to Install It*.

From the start it was a nip and tuck battle. We bought the wrong electric wire. Food funds ran low. But we learned to make do. Any steel I could find— including a Model T running board—went into the fireplace for reinforcing. Two thin trees, joined with bed slats, became a much-needed ladder. We nailed so many pieces of packing crates into the rough kitchen that we dubbed the place "Morrill's Scrap House."

One urgent problem was to find a way to keep our pipes from freezing. I had been warned that the waterline was buried only two feet deep and that the seventy-yard stretch to our spring would harden and break.

"You'll be melting snow for house water before New Year's," said one cynic, "and by Easter, when the pipe thaws, you'll have a sprinkling system."

I walked the line, however, and found that it went through our swamp. Somewhere I had read that swamps don't freeze. So we decided to chance it—which was all we could do anyhow. But where the line emerged from the ground under the house and branched off for bathroom and kitchen, we had to try some kind of protection. Here only the paper barrier would hold out subarctic blasts.

I sent to Sears-Roebuck for two lead-encased heat cables—$14.80, a serious investment. Crawling through cold dirt, I wrapped them around all exposed pipe. Then I wound rags and tar paper over them. Connected to our power system (if we ever got it installed), they would keep the pipes from freezing —unless the electricity conked out, which was freely predicted on all sides.

Visitors looked in, puzzled but friendly. "Winter jumped quick," said Richard Bradley. "Only six weeks ago, mosquitoes flew past my house carrying a sunstruck robin." He brought us some eggs, but was so scrupulously polite, wiping his feet again and again before stepping in, that I knew he considered us mere summer folk. True Vermonters, we had noticed, strode everywhere in muddy boots and growled amiable insults at the world.

"We'll have to earn our pedigree up here," I said.

Meanwhile, the mountain changed. Its rose-and-gold carpet vanished in shiny porcelain.

"It *is* a switch from the apartment," said Phyllis, now eight months along and moving more slowly. "We're so alone."

22

But that very morning a deer lifted velvet-brown ears at us from the birches. Next day a raccoon waded sleepily through the brook. Red squirrels pried orange halves from our frozen garbage and tucked them high in the maple trees—gay colored caches of vitamin C. We raised our coffee mugs to the frosty windows. We weren't alone at all.

Now minutes became gems. Could we burrow in before the first real blizzard? "We should be scared stiff, but there isn't time," I said.

The mysteries of construction seem to fade when you are in the wilderness—you *have* to do something. In the predawn dark, I mounted the chimney scaffold with cement and stones. At night, chattering with cold, I crawled under the floor and strung the power system. Phyllis pulled wires from the other end, shouting instructions from the book.

"When we throw the switch, I'm wearing sneakers," she said.

On weekends a muscular young Vermonter, Al Williams, came to help. He cost $1.25 an hour, a large item in our budget. But he was worth it—and then some. Together we tore old bricks from a collapsed cellar hole, soaked them in water, and slapped them into the fireplace.

Overalled men at Fuller Hardware in Saxtons River would listen patiently, then suggest moves. We used an oil drum for a workbench, a barn beam for a mantel. An ugly Victorian bed, given free at an auction, went four ways—metal into the concrete, legs into the stove, mattress against a chilly wall, headboard into the roof of a storage lean-to.

Our survival motto, borrowed from a World War II slogan, read: *Use it up. Wear it out. Make it do.*

Saw. Hammer. Mix mortar. Bit by bit we learned an ancient truth: Anxiety disappears if you keep in action. Weary at night, we sat by the roaring stove.

23

Phyllis read to Pete while the Coleman lantern hissed. I should have worried about the shrinking woodpile or the coming baby—but I just blew on my hot tomato soup. We slept like sacks of sand.

The next month brought victory and defeat. I scrounged $139 for a small floor furnace (Sears Winter Catalog). Electricity arrived and flowed into our one-bulb fixtures without a single short circuit. We installed a party-line phone.

But when I bought a load of wood, the truck broke through our bridge. Eight inches of snow fell, and Phyllis began having labor pains. I piled planks and sheet metal on the sagging bridge, then packed Phyllis and Pete in the car. Gingerly we crossed the bridge and raced to the hospital.

In less than a week, our overworked M.D. sent her back with Mike, a rubbery seven-pounder. Her mother arrived from Connecticut to lend a hand. She made the bunks, washed diapers, and was heroically cheerful. (Only years later would she admit that she cried most of the way back to Connecticut after her two-week stay.)

Now snow-twisters slammed down. Vermont's arctic vise had closed at last. In the nick of time I finished the fireplace and built a triumphant, howling blaze.

I had to ski down the mountain and bring up food by knapsack. Icicles—four-foot monsters—grew in our windows. At night we looked out through these glittering fangs at the moon grinning on a mad, white-turreted landscape.

I installed the floor furnace. As I wondered how to get a teacup of fuel, Richard Bradley drove up in a log sled, his big gray horses, Lexie and Prince, smoking at the nostrils. Si Finch rolled off six drums of kerosene.

"Should see you through—if you don't git drinking

it," the old farmer said. "And Cota and Cota won't bill you till March."

That evening Phyllis fed the baby by the fire and watched Pete play with his pine-scrap blocks. "I think we're going to make it," she said.

Even though the temperature dropped to 25-below and several chickadees froze on their branches, inside our cocoon warmth and light blossomed. I hooked up a secondhand water heater. In awe, we waded in a tub billowing with steam clouds. "Baths every night!" And to make the luxury more delectable, we ventured out each day, storm or no.

A congealed world, silent and milky, scented with evergreen, welcomed us. Far below, threads of smoke rose from Saxtons River. In brilliant sunlight, I tossed Pete into the drifts. He struggled to the surface unhurt, holding up his arms for more.

Gradually we grew attuned to the wild. The quiet mountain, we discovered, was actually bursting with noise. There were the rattle of ice-coated branches, the *glug-a-glug* of brook water, the *whoomf* of snow sliding off bent hemlocks. Once we heard the blood-chilling *screeeeeeeeeeeeeech* of a bobcat. Later I found yam-colored tufts of fur under an oak—evidence of forest strife that only the acorns will remember.

After each excursion we paused to hear wind whine in our electric wire. This blessed umbilical cord, looping down the mountain, siphoned our nourishment from civilization.

January . . . February. A pipe froze, a storm door blew apart. But we were sailing now. We weren't even fazed when in March our jeep broke an axle and money ran out. I went back to Z Persons at the bank, fingering my wool cap.

"Poaching any deer up there?" he said—and lent us another $500.

Rich again, we fixed the jeep and sheathed the liv-

25

ing room in knotty pine. Phyllis discovered Vermont church sales and reclothed us in used sweaters for a dollar apiece.

Then, without warning, winter collapsed. One morning Phyllis stood in the door, inhaling. "Mmmm—the south wind." For two weeks the mountain was afloat. Day and night the brook bellowed. Then the road appeared, bright with mud. And sweet fragrances drifted back—the tang of moist sod, a hint of trillium. This was our spring, earned in a fair fight.

A cross-valley farmer raced up on his tractor, sniffing out the new season. He leaned down while Richard Bradley and I toed the leathery ruts. We all cussed the road commissioner for not bringing gravel, and complained about taxes. The farmer said, "You boys winter on this godforsaken mountain? Lonely, ain't it?"

He thundered off. Richard Bradley snorted, "*Godforsaken!* That young snapper couldn't see through a barbed wire fence."

I said, "His crummy tractor has a piston-slap."

I was one of those half-mud, half-growl guys now. I was a Vermonter—or at least the beginnings of one.

So were Phyllis and Pete, come to think of it. She thrust her hands under my face.

"Look—calluses," she said.

I felt the hardened bumps in her palms. One fingernail was broken, one thumb bruised bright purple.

"You're gitting that backcountry, calico look, Marthy. Any minute you might run out and start hanging sap buckets."

She placed a forefinger on her temple. "No calluses up here, Zeke. *Yet.*"

Her cheeks had grown red and healthy. Her eyes

26

were as radiant as sapphires. Pete was changed, too—a bit stronger, a bit more swaggery. In one season they had toughened, like transplants adapting to the Arctic.

"Throw Mike some birch bark to chew, will you?" I said.

Where the People Rule

IN THE NEXT six months we got to know our territory and its people.

Westminster, where we paid our taxes ($26 a year), had a proud history. The township was where Vermont had declared itself a republic on January 15, 1777. Remaining a sovereign nation for fourteen years, it had finally joined the Union as the fourteenth state.

In Westminster's ancient cemetery lies the body of William French, killed while resisting Royal authority more than a month before the Battle of Lexington. The patriot's epitaph reads:

> Here William French his Body lies
> For murder his blood for Vengance cries
> King George the third his Tory crew
> tha with a bawl his head Shot threw
> For Liberty and His Country's Good
> he Lost his Life his Dearest blood.

Phyllis and I touched the roughhewn words wonderingly, and later a friend made us a rubbing of them for our wall.

Westminster was our legal home. But since our house was cut off from it by an impassable mountain road, we looked on Saxtons River, two miles to our north, as our real town. There we bought food at Mac's Grocery, dickered with Stanley Adams at the hardware store, and secured our mail. What couldn't be found in Saxtons River might be picked up in the larger village of Bellows Falls, four miles to the east.

Bellows Falls (which barnyard sports called "Fellows Balls") was a metropolis to us and everyone else within twenty miles. It had about four thousand people. Choked with brick storefronts and old paper mills, it claimed cachet as a Saturday night oasis. It had a movie theater, a couple of department stores, an ice-cream parlor, a firehouse, some service businesses, and three banks that lent very little money. On weekends the sidewalks echoed with farmers' boots and occasional high heels.

The town hugged the Connecticut River where the water dropped precipitously. These waterfalls—long since tamed by a power dam—had once been a natural marvel. An unknown Englishman, visiting them in 1781, wrote:

Two hundred miles from the [Connecticut] Sound is a narrow of five yards only, formed by two shelving mountains of solid rock. Through this chasm are compelled to pass all the waters which, in time of floods, bury the northern country. Here the water is consolidated, without frost, by pressure, as it swiftly passes through the pinching, sturdy rocks. . . . The passage is about 400 yards in length, in a zigzag form with obtuse corners. Timber and trees strike on one side or the other, and are rent in one moment into shivers and splintered . . . to the amazement of the spectator.

29

No living creature was ever known to pass through this narrow except an Indian woman, who was in a canoe, attempting to cross the river above it, but carelessly let herself fall within the power of the current. Perceiving her danger, she took a bottle of rum she had with her, and drank the whole of it, then lay down in her canoe to meet her destiny. She miraculously went through safe, and was taken out of the canoe intoxicated.

Throughout history Indians had valued the falls as a good place to spear fish. Even before the tribes faded, white men had filtered in, likewise attracted to the scenic riverbank.

The white settlers threw up log cabins and slowly built a township called Rockingham. (Today Rockingham embraces the villages of Bellows Falls and Saxtons River.) It was a rough community, appealing to frontier-type people. Blizzards, loneliness, and brutal work took a toll. But these pioneers enjoyed a broad river to float timber on. And, inland from the falls, their axes could bite into lush forests of oak and hemlock. So they stuck. Some prospered, and these, of necessity, set up stern laws to hold their big-muscled brethren in check.

For wrongdoers, Rockingham had stocks and pillory, along with other crude methods of punishment common to most Vermont towns. (As late as 1804, Westminster boasted two whipping posts.) A typical statute read:

Whosoever shall commit burglary ... shall, for the first offense, be branded on the forehead with the capital letter B, with a hot iron, and shall have one of his ears nailed to a post and cut off; and shall also be whipped on the naked body 15 stripes.

A second offense brought more whipping and the loss of the other ear. A third brought death.

Intoxication, cursing, horse stealing, and blasphemy were punished with severe lashing.

The township also employed the device of "warning out of town" any newcomers who looked as if they couldn't pay their way. As far back as 1769, Rockingham's founders, fearful that they might have to support ne'er-do-well immigrants, voted "that all Strangers who Com to Inhabit in said town Not freeholders be warned out of town."

Thus, solid citizens were relieved of tapping their hard-earned revenue for the poor. As it turned out, many persons who received this humiliating warning wouldn't budge and gradually became property owners and even town officials.

Later, the care of paupers was sold at auction to the lowest bidder. In one case a helpless "Mrs. Burr" was advertised and bid off by "John Roundy at five shillings a week." Presumably he fed and sheltered her for that fee.

Hard people shaped by hard conditions, these early Rockingham folk cleared the land and hacked out the roads that the Morrills' jeep now bounced over. I found it difficult to fault them; indeed, I was awed by their effort. They built dams and set up sawmills. They lugged stone. In the mid-1800s they pushed heavy flatboats on the river, the poles making calluses on their shoulders "as large as hands." When the railroad came through, they put their sinew to it also, cutting ties and laying track.

It is not surprising that a prickly independence grew among such people. It manifested itself down the years, sometimes in odd ways. Early in the nineteenth century, angry citizens blew up a five-foot dinosaur track on a ledge near the river rather than allow its removal to Dartmouth College.

This was the breed of settlers who, pushing back from the Connecticut River, founded Saxtons River in 1820. Eight years later, *Thompson's Gazetteer of Vermont* described the hamlet as having "an elegant meetinghouse, a post office, two carding machines, one grist, two saw, and fulling mills, one tannery, one forge, one furnace, one distillery, two woolen factories, one tavern, two stores, one law office, and 45 dwelling places."

So Saxtons River—our real hometown—had had a bustling start. And the relics of this energetic period lurked in the sleepy, paint-peeling buildings that lined Main Street. The village that we knew was a weather-worn place, drowsing in the memory of more prosperous times. It had a couple of struggling sawmills, a small woodworking factory, two garages, an Odd Fellows Hall, and a pair of big churches that the congregations could not afford to maintain.

A squarish Victorian hotel sat in the middle, across from Fuller Hardware. The hotel, too, was run down, its porch sagging. The post office occupied half of an A & P grocery, and all day long rust-pocked cars, log trucks, and tractors—green John Deeres and red International Harvesters—came and went there.

Main street had once been overarched with graceful elms. It had even boasted a trolley line to Bellows Falls. But now the trees were mostly gone and the trolley rails were just healed scars in the roadbed. Chunks of log bark lay in the gutters. Looking at the street's patched roofs and bumpy sidewalks, its seedy storefronts and time-haunted fence posts brought to mind the phrase "workingman's town." If ever there was a summer-blistered, winter-blasted Vermont backwater, this was it.

Back from Main Street, however, frame houses straggled toward the hills, and they were full of friendly, invigorating people. They worked in Springfield tool factories, drove truck for St. Johnsbury Express, gardened a little, carpentered a little, saved their money, and paid their taxes. Many of them ran small businesses, from saw sharpening to radio repair. They were extraordinarily capable of taking care of themselves.

Furthermore, they had a strong sense of history. Go into a Saxtons River house and you were likely to run into an *Encyclopaedia Britannica* tucked amid the fishing rods and rifles. Years later, when the Saxtons River Historical Society got going, village attics were to disgorge an astounding trove of memorabilia. There were tinsmith tools, carefully saved from another age. There were parlor stoves, built from the soapstone of a nearby quarry. Ancient family Bibles, 100-year-old gowns, homemade toys, locally manufactured clocks with wooden works—everything poured out, a cornucopia of Time.

What gave the place its heart, however, and put the lie to any idea of decline, was its children—and the grown-ups' attitude toward them. Saxtons River teemed with kids. Red-faced gamins carrying baseball bats or dolls overflowed on the lawns and streets. They chewed bubble gum and rode bikes. They tumbled out of the back of pickup trucks. They did old-fashioned things such as going to taffy pulls and holding foot races. In summer, they scampered, giggling, at the band concerts held outside the hotel.

Kids were everywhere. Grown-ups accepted them as they accepted rainbows, taxes, and measles—facts of life to be enjoyed and endured. Few Saxtons River barns were not crammed with tennis rackets, catchers' masks, balls, skis, toboggans, creels, tricycles, and every other conceivable piece of sports equipment. The stuff might be old and long used but, at the appropriate time, out it came onto the playing slopes and fields.

Grown-ups might seem casual about their underfoot, always clambering progeny. But they appeared to have an absolute horror of any child's going without skis, sled, or skates in winter—if he wanted them. Each year church groups put on a giant swap session at which outgrown equipment was traded for the right size. Thus if a new Flexible Flyer entered the Saxtons River family circle, it was liable to circulate there until its runners wore off. Kids careening around ice ponds recognized the racing tubulars they had used last year. Often they also recognized sweaters and mittens they had worn, for rummage sales kept good clothes revolving economically within the community.

In sum, Saxtons River's attitude toward its young was one of affection without indulgence. Nobody was hesitant about hugging or spanking his child in public if the moment asked for it. Youth was respectful of age—to a point. And the whole community looked with pride on a son who earned an Air Force commission or merited a tryout with the Red Sox.

The key to this easy-working relationship was a mutual love of outdoor activity. Fathers liked to hunt and fish, so they brought their sons along. They liked baseball, skiing, hiking, archery, and white-water kayaking and so did the sons. If daughters showed inclinations of this sort, they too joined in. Years before Women's Lib, Saxtons River girls were tomboying with a vengeance. Some became crack shots and skilled horse riders, and they kept up their interest the rest of their lives. Others went into the woods and cut timber with their men.

One day Phyllis called me into the tiny enclave I had built as a nursery.

"This is your son, Michael Lee," she said. "Mike, here's your Old Man."

I looked at the chubby, waving hands. Sunk in his soft blue blanket, Mike was a cherub by Titian. He had merry eyes and pink, heart-shaped lips.

"We've met before," I said.

"Not really."

Phyllis went on to say that I barely knew my second son. I had been hammering and cementing at all hours. I was up at five pecking the typewriter. I was away at Chester during the week. Saturdays and Sundays were gone in a haze of labor.

"If there's anything I've noticed about Saxtons River," she said, "it's that parents take time out to know their kids."

I picked Mike up. He looked surprised. Then he gurgled—and grinned.

"He's such a *good* baby," Phyllis added softly. "You'll like each other."

That afternoon I built a six-inch boat out of pine. I sanded the edges, set the brads in an eighth of an inch, and puttied the holes. I dropped it in Mike's crib, and he examined it gravely.

Thereafter, when Phyllis washed him (in the kitchen sink) the boat had to be there, bobbing around in the soapy water. It was the first of dozens of homemade wooden things he came to love.

Mike seemed to get a real boot out of construction. At night when I sawed knotty-pine lengths for the walls, he peered through his crib bars. As soon as his hands were strong enough, they reached for the hammer handle. He crawled for tools, then toddled with them.

Pete showed him how to build with blocks, how to knock everything down and start over again. Before he could talk, Mike was constructing garages for toy trucks.

"I'm going to try an experiment," I told Phyllis.

I put a small hammer, a few nails, and some scrap lumber beside Mike as he napped. He awoke and went to work—pounding wood together, tapping his thumb and crying now and then, but refusing to stop.

"From now on," I said, "I'll keep tools and nails within reach of both kids. In a few years, I'll bet they'll be teaching me how to do it."

I did that. In time both Pete and Mike grew accustomed to making things. I paid a heavy price in lost tools (an *agonizing* price in the early days when a screwdriver had to double as a chisel). But I began to feel like a Vermont father, an active patriarch helping his bairns grow up by themselves.

"Up here," said Phyllis, "a lot of old-fashioned virtues still work. Mothers and fathers have *teaching* duties. The family is more important than the state."

Sure enough, I noticed that Vermonters usually put people ahead of everything else, including conventional customs and some laws. They wanted their children to grow up in their midst, involved in family affairs.

Above all, they wanted them independently minded.

This spirit of independence, in fact, was both the glory and despair of the state. It stuck with the young after they became adults. It was the spirit that in 1850 had caused an outraged General Assembly to reject the newly enacted U.S. Fugitive Slave Law and to declare that any escaped black who reached the Vermont border was free. It was also the murkier spirit that prompted some men to shoot deer out of season and to hide cows so they couldn't be taxed.

One day, on the outskirts of town, I bought some lumber from a grizzled old sawyer. He figured out my board feet on the back of a cereal box and added up the cost.

I examined the numbers. "You forgot the state sales tax," I said.

He looked at me in surprise, and I could see the thorny freedom teachings of long ago rise up.

"Fuck the state," he said.

Stumbling Around in Business

BY THE SECOND SUMMER we had a toehold on the mountain. I built some solid new stairs to our small attic and spread two mattresses there. If anyone was fool enough to visit us, we had accommodations. Phyllis planted some flowers in old iron kettles and perched them on stumps outside.

My boss, Albert Boni, came to supper and hiked around the property. "Nice," he said in his clipped way. "But why so far from Chester? Why so far from your work?" He ran a unique company. He liked his people living close to it.

Readex produced print so small that it couldn't be read with an ordinary magnifying glass. A page of *The New York Times* could be reduced to the size of a postage stamp. The purpose behind this was the easy and economical storage of reading matter, as well as the scholarly assemblage of research materials.

The main project was the printing of the British Sessional Papers, the day-by-day records of the House of Commons from its very beginning centuries ago. It was a monster of a job, involving the collating and miniaturization of vast numbers of pages. Most of the filming was done with the collection of originals in the New York Public Library. Some was done in England, although war bombing had destroyed many records over there (which was one reason for putting together complete sets as replacements).

Other projects included the total UN Assembly records, U.S. Patent Office data, and the *Complete British and American Plays*.

Microprint came on a card, 5 by 9 inches in measure. Usually one card carried 100 pages of original text, each reduced to the size of a thumbnail. The cards could be read in a machine that magnified each page at the flip of a dial—a marvelous assemblage of lenses and lights that Albert Boni himself had invented.

For purposes of examination during work, we had to bend over microprint with a 10x glass, like a jeweler fixing a watch. The Lilliputian print flared up at us, clear as crystal.

Poring over these tiny copies of ancient documents, we sometimes encountered bizarre scraps of information. Once I read a *Report on the Condition of the Prisoners in the Hulks at Woolwich*, horrifying revelations of the eighteenth-century English penal practices. Page after page told of human hands, feet, entrails, and heads being dumped overboard by bucket, of whippings and chainings.

Again, I read with surprise a play in original penmanship by Johnny Burgoyne, the debonair British general who came a cropper at the Battle of Saratoga. His effort was only one of thousands in the *Complete British and American Plays*.

Microprint was a revolutionary process. Although film was used in part of the manufacturing routine, the final product was ink on paper. Thus it could be produced relatively cheaply. And it would last for decades, even centuries.

Since all other micropublications boiled down to film, in rolls or on cards, everyone was amazed that microprint could use ink. One smudge the size of birdseed would blot out a whole paragraph. If the ink was a mite too runny, entire pages would become blobs. Yet microprint was—and is—readable in libraries all over the world.

In truth, a remarkable product developed by a remarkable man. Albert Boni, I learned the first week I worked for him, was an old New York publisher. In the twenties he and his brother had introduced paperbacks to drugstores—Bonibooks, they were called. Before that he had been a correspondent in revolutionary Russia, where he had once been imprisoned by the Bolsheviks. He had known, and had usually battled with, most of the literary luminaries of the post-World War I era, from Ernest Hemingway to Theodore Dreiser.

My job was to run Readex's lone press on the lower floor. Since our plant was an old mortuary, an aura of timelessness pervaded the high-ceilinged rooms—the place *smelled* ancient. My boss was Werner Theilheimer, a young redhead of considerable brilliance who had helped Albert refine the microprinting process. His title was Plant Manager. There were five other members of the firm, all women. One, Ruth Balch, was secretary, and the others worked on photographic strips that preceded the conversion of film into print.

Werner, a New Yorker who played the flute, was already fed up with Vermont. "Desolation Unlimited," he called it. Soon after we became friends and he saw the remoteness of my cabin, he gave me a rifle for defense against marauders.

Werner had a sense of humor. Down cellar at the

plant, he found a gallon of what I consider the most aptly named product of all time—Zero Embalming Fluid—and parked it on his desk.

"If anybody starts moving too fast around here," he said, "give him a shot of it."

Again, riding the rope elevator that had once hoisted bodies and coffins from floor to floor, he observed that progress was the natural state of man. "This rig now carries only *living* corpses," he said.

From Werner, I learned that Albert Boni was very much worried about someone's stealing the Readex process.

"He holds back things from me, even," he said. "He takes the plates home and gives them his special secret processing before we can use them." He gave me a broad wink.

The plates were chemically treated surfaces, mailed every few weeks from a New York plant. They were a standard product for offset printing, but Albert insisted that only he open each package in his private laboratory, so he could apply his unique magic to them. Werner had long since discovered that Albert did nothing to the plates, but he went along with the charade, if a bit scornful of this passion for secrecy.

"Albert is holding his cards so close to his chest," he said, "that he can't see what he's got."

I learned also that Readex was nearly broke. When, after thirty days, I asked for my agreed raise, Albert's brow arched up.

"Sixty dollars, sixty dollars?" he said. "What's this?"

He couldn't remember agreeing to a thing. But I would not retreat. Finally he gave in, shrugging. "I must have been cuckoo," he said, walking out of the pressroom.

As time passed, I grew used to the changing seasons on the road to Chester. New employees were hired and fired. Finally Werner went back to New York, and I became Plant Manager, still at my princely sixty-dollar wage.

Gradually I got to know Albert. He had the hardihood and intensity that go with genius. He could make wise, generous moves, and he could quibble over trifles. Once he gave me some stunning Russian posters of 1917 that he had casually stored in the attic. I exclaimed over them—huge color caricatures of Red soldiers chasing fat, top-hatted U.S. capitalists, factory workers waving banners, and so on. He agreed that they were unusual, then took them back and sent them to a museum.

Again, he brought Pete and Mike a bale of candy figurines, then delivered a sharp complaint about the way wastebaskets were distributed around the plant.

One week, when he was in New York, we received a much needed shipment of plates. Their lack had held up production for two days, so I started using them, despite Ruth Balch's warning that Mr. Boni had to process them first.

The phone rang. "What are you doing up there?" asked Albert.

"The press is going again," I said.

"I thought you were out of plates."

"Some came in."

"Stop the press! I haven't processed those plates."

"They're running perfectly."

"Stop the press!"

We shut down. For the next three days we polished and painted the plant. Then Albert returned, took the plates to his house, and hurried back with them. We began to roll once more.

"Nell and I have our crotchets," he admitted.

Nell was his Dutch wife, an intelligent, unselfish lady who spoke with a delightful accent. She knew the business well enough to handle the filming end of it—and eventually did in New York. She also knew

42

how to cook. Her dinners, served on an antique Colonial table, beguiled the nostrils and warmed the taste buds.

The Boni marriage was solid, an inspiration to a younger couple such as Phyllis and me. And full of frank exchanges.

"Yoo are such a son-uf-a-beech, Albert," she said to him mildly one night when we were guests.

"I know it—but they don't," he replied, and went on talking to Phyllis.

By this time I was doing everything under the sun at Readex—running the press, handling correspondence, ordering supplies, painting the floor, and helping wrap shipments. Occasionally I would have to talk creditors out of taking drastic measures against the company. One day an irate owner of a lens firm showed up, threatening to put a lien on the plant. We had owed him several hundred dollars for eight months. He raged around the office while I tried to talk soothingly. After he left, I called Albert in New York. If I expected him to be alarmed, I was far off the mark.

"To hell with him," he said, "Let me handle the bastard."

I never heard any more about it.

The incident pointed up Albert's obsession, which was his great strength. He was absolutely determined that nothing would stop the development of his invention. He was surprised—and even outraged—when others didn't display the same kind of devotion.

One day he decided that I would work nights and Saturdays to get the production up. I refused. I was unwilling to leave a wife and two small children marooned on a snow-wedged mountain for longer hours.

Albert grew angry. I expected to be fired. But he walked around, arguing. For the first time he talked

43

about the financial situation, which had just taken a new, perilous turn. "This place is all I've got," he said. "This is all I have to leave to Nell."

His voice was strained, his face taut—and suddenly I began to like Albert Boni very much. He was an embattled Vermonter like the rest of us. He had flung all his resources, spiritual and material, into an idea. Nearing his sixties, he had worked compulsively in his house, experimenting at all hours with inks, plates, and printing presses. Advised that a machine to enlarge microprint to readable size was optically impossible, he had invented one anyhow, although at the start he had known nothing about optics. And he had fought off the wolves of competition that I knew little about. He was quite a guy.

"I'll work at noon when we need it," I said.

We did get the production up. The crisis was averted. Others came, of course (for one three-week stretch I received no pay and lived on grocery store credit), but Readex grew. We built a fireproof storage house, added another press, hired more help.

And after strenuous parleys with Albert, I got my salary up to $85 a week.

I also got new insights into my fascinating boss. I went swimming with him in a small river behind his house. He spent the whole time feeling for smooth stones with his feet. When he found one, he would duck under, heave it up, and lug it to a big sievelike dam stretching from bank to bank.

"I build this dam every summer," he said. "The fall rains wash it out, but then I put it back."

Finally, he and Nell sold their house and went to New York permanently—leaving me to wrestle with Readex alone. Thereafter, when he came to Vermont for a business weekend, he stayed at my house. Here, he really let go. Sometimes Phyllis and the kids would be away in Connecticut. Albert would strip to his underwear, grab an ax, and hack away at the stumps around the cabin. We cooked supper on the outside fireplace and talked over beer and coffee to all hours.

Albert, I learned, had quit Harvard as an undergraduate to become a publisher. He had put out books by authors ranging from Thornton Wilder and Marcel Proust to Nan Britton, the mother of President Harding's illegitimate daughter. He had been deep in the intellectual ferment of the time. One of the first Westerners to get into Russia after the 1917 Revolution, he had written articles predicting a Stalinist-style dictatorship there.

"Once in the early days," he said, "I met Lenin under funny circumstances—and ended up in jail the next week."

He had been in a railroad station with a Russian acquaintance, lamenting the fact that he could not get into a Workers' Convention about to be convened.

"But you can," said the Russian, pinning a badge on him. "I'm making you a delegate."

A train chugged in, bearing Red guards with rifles. A bell clanged. Unexpectedly, Lenin stepped out of a rear car. Before the receiving party could reach him, he seized Albert's and the Russian's hands and said, "March with me to the convention hall."

Up the street they marched, the conqueror of the czars flanked by an obscure countryman and an American bourgeois. A dozen rows back, seething with frustration, walked John Reed, the American Communist. The first movie cameras were grinding, and for months thereafter newsreels everywhere would feature the scene.

"John Reed was a friend," said Albert. "But I think he got me arrested."

A few days later there was a knock on Albert's hotel room door. Two big soldiers escorted him to prison.

"Reed probably told them I was bourgeois, and they took no chances with capitalist plotters around Lenin."

In jail, Albert refused to work, as other prisoners were required to do. He read books and waited. Meanwhile, friends, hearing of his plight, raised loud noises with the authorities, both U.S. and Russian. Finally, Albert was carried by sealed train to the Polish border and dumped out.

Those were good sessions, that long summer—with potatoes, tossed in the fire, cooking to a swarthy black and coffee *put-putting* in the percolator. Twilight dropped crimson shafts through the trees. Sweet scents blew from the valley. After a while, our windows turned to golden pools, and all of Vermont seemed to fall into a dream. Albert and I usually stayed out until the stars winked on. After the birds had stopped their soft flutings, and a couple of distant barks had put a final exclamation point to conversation, we went inside—and yakked on.

Woofs, Hoots, and Other Vibrations

October, 1950, is here, I wrote in my notebook, *and last night a rain storm ripped all the color out of the trees.*

The beautiful autumn, so looked forward to on our mountain, was gone almost the moment it arrived. To make matters worse, I had run out of plywood for the ceilings and could buy no more. Things had taken a gloomy turn at Readex—production off, wages held up.

Tight times, I wrote. *Well, something will happen. . . .*

That afternoon Phyllis met a girl standing outside Mac's Grocery. She was holding a brown puppy on the end of a frazzled rope and was nearly in tears.

"My mother won't let me keep him," she said. "Will you take him?"

The pup cocked a ragged brown ear. He had a roguish grin, a tail splashed with white. In the jeep he chewed the bottom off three food bags before Phyllis got to the gate.

47

Pete and dog embraced. "He's got a tail like a feather," he cried. "I want to call him Feather."

Feather cheered us. What could go wrong when a rollicking dog was in the cabin, chewing shoes, yanking sheets through Mike's crib?

Answer: everything. Feather knocked a dish off the table, ate half a chicken left temporarily on the counter, and made a mess on the rug. Indignant, Phyllis shooed him out the door.

Within two hours he was back whining. Pete looked out.

"He's got things sticking in his face, and he's shaking his head!"

He was loaded with porcupine quills. Phyllis, Pete, and I wrestled him onto his back, rammed a branch into his jaws to hold them open, and used pliers to pull out the sharp black-and-white points. Some of the needles had gone clean through his tongue.

He growled, yiped, squirmed. Pete wept and I cursed. Finally it was over, and he scrambled up, wagging his plumelike tail. Blood dripped from his mouth.

"He's going to be a hell raiser."

The next day Richard Bradley appeared at the door. Had we seen a limber little pup, sort of caramel-colored? It had killed one of his chickens.

Phyllis grimaced. "I picked a murderer."

Richard laughed it off. He stayed for coffee. This small, sharp-featured old man maintained a philosophic slant on catastrophes. Born in Liverpool, he clung proudly to his overseas citizenship (although he had lived here long enough to be considered the Old Man of the Mountain), and he displayed typical English calm.

"I had a dog once who used to bite horses," he said.

He regaled us with dog stories and made us feel

48

better. Phyllis got down the nickel-and-penny jar to pay for the chicken, but he wouldn't hear of it.

"Been wanting a chicken dinner anyhow," he said. "By jeez, that pup is going to be something if he can run down a hen at his age."

Weeks passed. Feather sprouted long, muscular legs. He was all mountain dog. He chased the cats and fought a pitched battle with Franklin D. Roosevelt, suffering a lacerated nose but driving the outraged feline up a tree. He began to vanish for days at a time. Once I made the mistake of locking him in the house. When we got back from a day trip, he had torn open seven cement bags stored in the living room and flung the pieces over everything. He had also chewed off part of the door.

Discipline simply did not work with this outlaw—although we tried. After he tore apart a laundry bag or ripped open the garbage, he would submit without protest to a switching, then bark joyfully and lope into the woods.

Before long he became the World's Most Lethal Watchdog. When the electric company's pickup bounced onto the Flat, Feather's deep growl would begin. His shoulder fur would puff out a full three inches. The meter man would roll down the window nervously.

"That hound tied up?"

I would slap a chain on Feather's rawhide collar. I would hold him—and cuss him until the truck roared off.

Such an antisocial animal was bound to have collisions with the outside world. He was death to all foreign cats—and would scatter our own when he felt restive. Snoozing by the fire, nose between his paws, he draped his tail affectionately across the foot of one of us. But, slinking through the hemlocks, he always zeroed his cold black eyes in on a target.

49

It was no surprise to me when one night he dragged himself home, trailing blood, his chest and right front leg crushed.

"I heard him yelp," said Richard Bradley, one of the few persons outside the family who got along with Feather. "Log truck. He always chases them and bites the tires. One of them mean boys swung the wheel on him."

Feather wouldn't die. He lay on a rug near the hearth and wagged his tail feebly. We ministered to him as if he were battle-wounded royalty. I tried to set the bones, but his whole chest seemed caved in. Going to a veterinarian was out of the question. The Readex payroll had failed again, and we were barely able to buy food.

Everyone who looked at him told us to shoot him, but we would not. Then one morning he struggled to his feet, whimpering. He circled the room, now and then giving a yelp of pain. He held his crushed leg to his chest.

For several days he ritually went through this exercise. He stopped yelping. He drank a full bowl of milk. I got a meaty bone and kept a fresh newspaper under it on his rug. Finally, he went to the door and nudged it with his nose.

"He wants to go out!" cried Pete.

We watched him limp up the Flat, a three-legged cripple. Suddenly a chipmunk shot past. Feather's ears made pyramids. He dived for the gold-and-black rodent—and collapsed, howling.

Phyllis burst into tears.

For several weeks Feather looked like a hobbling clothes rack. But he kept in motion. He began to eat. His body filled out. We saw him running experimentally, holding the ruined limb to his chest.

He was permanently deformed. By January, however, he had developed a three-pronged leg movement that yielded astonishing speed. One day he brought me a woodchuck he had killed and stood back, his tail flopping wildly.

Throughout the winter this extraordinary animal trained himself to his new condition. As drifts covered Little Baldy, he made trails consisting of jump-spots six feet apart. He would leap from one to another. After each snowfall, we would see him criss-crossing the mountain, keeping the route open.

I tried to keep his bad leg active by rubbing the muscles. But he could not move it from its chest position, and gradually it atrophied. The other three legs bulged all the larger with steely sinew.

Spring, 1951, brought us a new, crazy-gaited Feather just as sassy and insolent as the old. He could stalk, run, and leap like a lynx. His stamina was phenomenal. He went back to chasing log trucks and slashing porcupines. Once again I had to tie him whenever we drove away, for he was fast enough to run all the way to Saxtons River, yelping at the exhaust—and we were afraid his heart would explode.

Always he chewed through the Manila line within four minutes anyway, so we weren't abridging his precious freedom by much.

From then on, Feather was Gimp Lord of the Mountain. Strangers and stray dogs kept their distance.

One morning, when Feather was off on a half-week excursion, a little waif of a dog, tan-and-white, appeared on the Knoll. He was half-paralyzed, nodding his head and snapping at air involuntarily. Phyllis brought him milk in a dish. He tried to drink, tried to wag his tail, but he was helpless. I got him to our lean-to. He would not stay, but struggled out onto the road.

There he stood for hours, snapping. Collarless, bedraggled, he was a symbol of everything forlorn on

51

earth. In the morning I found him semiconscious, covered with frost. I shot him with my .22 and buried him on the Knoll.

This killing was a reminder that a country man had an obligation to be an agent of death sometimes—a part of life's cycle. A thoughtful person got no joy out of it, but he couldn't flee the duty.

A few days later, driving to town, I had to steer around a raccoon blinking in the sun. I stopped to examine him. He was obviously sick. Any wild animal that will not flinch from a human can be dangerous—rabid, perhaps. My duty was to eliminate him, but I shrank from it.

I told myself, *If he's still here when I get back, I'll take care of him.* Hours later, I returned and saw with relief that the road was empty. But as I passed, the snout of the raccoon glinted in the bushes. He had moved less than four feet. I killed him with one blow of a baseball bat and buried him in a ditch.

Phyllis and I talked it over. With violent death all around us—from snakes eating frogs to wildcats killing rabbits—it seemed finicky to be troubled about delivering a lethal blow. It didn't bother a lot of people. But we found ourselves reluctant to play God and decide when a creature—a miraculous assemblage of breathing, feeling chromosomes—must die.

"We'll be on the side of life," she said.

I recalled the time, early in the game, when I had been sleeping on the floor before a snapping stove fire. A field mouse hopped out of the kitchen. He stood on his hind legs and looked at me without fear. I flung a shoe at him, killing him instantly. It was a civilized reflex; mice don't belong in houses. But, looking at the tiny, blood-spattered corpse, I thought: *This is what's wrong with the universe. Without thinking, I attacked.*

Since then, I had never killed a field mouse. They

came in for the winter and went out for the summer. The cats policed them, limiting them to far niches of the walls. They didn't bother us; we didn't hassle them. Fair deal.

The new summer moved on, a yellow tide. Porcupines gnawed at the cabin's underpinning, and Feather tried to dig through our makeshift lower walls to reach them. One night when he was away, the chewing sounded as if the whole floor were being devoured.

"Ye gods, are they coming into the room?" said Phyllis.

"Enough of this baloney," I said.

I went after them with Coleman lantern and rifle. Somehow they got out from under the house, but I caught one heading for the woods. I pumped six .22 bullets into a waddling pincushion that kept tumbling and getting up. It got as far as the bushes, its quills streaming with cherry-colored blood.

It breathed like a bellows—and died.

By daylight, I examined the gnaw spots. The porcs were chewing only some loose boards that had once been flooring and were suffused with tasty oil. The hungry animals were after dessert, that's all.

"I've shot my last porcupine," I told Richard Bradley. "I am now the biggest sissy in southern Vermont."

He laughed. Then he told me about shooting a deer that kept raiding his garden. One night he got it with a single bullet. It was still twitching as he bent over it with a flashlight.

"The critter had a carrot right in its mouth," he said. "It rolled up its eyes at me like a human. I've never killed a deer since."

He was at ease with nature's equation, and I decided that the same posture would be good for us also. The rest of the summer he and I would meet on the Knoll to talk, often about farming or history. (Richard considered the American Revolution a tragedy that never should have happened.)

One Sunday he pointed his cane at some ink-black birds cavorting in his western field. "See them crows?" he said. "Having a time in my corn. Some folks don't like that, but I figure there's enough here for everybody. I just call crows 'my black hens' and let it go at that."

"He's got some of Schweitzer's idea—reverence for life," I told Phyllis.

"I like that."

So our family became viewers instead of hunters. Our quarry was the *incident* in the wild, the unexpected happening that made us wonder.

On Big Baldy I touched a long black snake with a stick to see what he would do. He wriggled madly. He shot up a big, smooth-barked beech like a ribbon on a barber pole, round and round. Twenty feet up he looped himself over a limb and looked down. I examined the tree. It was at least a foot thick, sleek as a pie pan. How had he gotten a grip on it with his slippery belly?

Again, I watched a field mouse berate a cat—and get away with it. Captured near our outside kindling box, he stood on his hind legs and squeaked angrily at his tormenter. The cat cuffed him. He tumbled, then *charged* the cat. Bop—the cat knocked him back. The mouse leaped up again, waving his front paws like a boxer.

For minutes the sequence continued. The cat punched. The mouse tumbled. Each time the mouse hopped, enraged and squeaking, he edged nearer the box. At last he scrambled up from a blow, delivered a final tirade, and let himself be knocked under the box—to freedom.

Had the mouse actually planned that strategy?

As October came around again, we looked with new, curious eyes on deer, foxes, beavers, hawks, wild ducks, and other mountain life. Owls *who-ooed* at night, a haunting sound. Feather growled in his spot by the fireplace.

One dark evening Pete and Mike, encased in red Dr. Denton pajamas, climbed into the kitchen sink and watched breathlessly while a raccoon went to work on our outside garbage cans. The coon had trouble with the covers. He pried at them with his humanlike paws. He hurt one paw, looked at it, sucked it, and shook it, like a fat, exasperated little man. Then he gave the offending can an angry slap and walked away from it.

But he stopped and looked back. He circled the cans. He tried the covers again. No luck. He stood on his hind legs and wrestled violently with one of the cans. At last he flung it over, and the cover popped off. He rubbed his paws in glee. Then he picked up the cover and hurled it away with scorn before he sorted through the pickings.

It was a vaudeville routine which, with music, would have been cheered on the New York stage: The Waltz of the Testy Old Man.

Wildlife kept pressing in on us. Our water began to taste gamy. I pushed back the concrete cover of our spring and found two chipmunk bodies floating a foot below the surface. They had scampered down a two-inch runoff pipe and fallen in. I fished them out and wired some screen over the pipe end.

Squirrels invaded our attic. Foxes shattered our sleep (how they barked!). Woodchucks burrowed in our field. But the stir of life around us gladdened our heart. Animal watching, we decided, was the country's best antidote to loneliness—and more than paid its keep.

Poor—or Just Dumb?

"WE are *not* poor," said Phyllis. "I reject the idea."

"We're just out of money," I said.

An early snow was falling. We were three years into our experiment. The cabin was finished on the inside—walls of sweet-smelling knotty pine. The kids slept in fresh, warm sheets. A rosy fire crackled.

The only trouble was that we were down to $1.75 again.

"We're doing something wrong," I said. "Four weeks ago I sold a story to *MEN*. Two hundred bucks. Where did it go?"

That was easy. We shuffled through a shoe box of receipts: Fuller Hardware, $67.75; Tenney's Lumber Mill, $37.80; Whitcomb Sand & Gravel, $49.30; O'Connor's Garage, $28.60. The rest had dribbled away on food, clothes, and a new toaster.

We pored over the year's spotty records. Then we raised our brows at each other.

"The bald truth is we can't keep building up this place and support a family on eighty-five bucks a week," I said.

56

"I'm getting a job," said Phyllis.

She would go teaching. Get a girl to live in as baby-sitter. We made a pot of coffee and argued about the idea. I was dubious.

"I'll start by getting on the sub list at Saxtons River school," she said, as we undressed for bed.

A few weeks later, however, she gave me a strange look. "I think I'm pregnant—nice going."

There went her economic game plan. But she had talked so enthusiastically about the coming upsurge in our fortunes that I couldn't bear to disappoint her.

"Let's push ahead anyhow," I said.

I got her to help me draw up some plans for enlarging the cabin. Our tiny kitchen was so jammed with secondhand water heater and washing machine that the back door couldn't be fully opened.

"We need some space here," I said.

Phyllis addressed the heavens. "Man here says we need space."

We listed the priorities: foundation with concrete blocks; storm windows and doors; enlarged kitchen; garage with extra room and bath; a breezeway to the garage; a culvert to replace the rickety bridge over our brook.

"Figure about three thousand bucks—if I do the jackass labor," I said.

"We'll donkey it together, Zeke."

I returned to Z Persons at the Brattleboro Bank and Trust. He mulled over our plans and said, "Mmmmmmm." Then he shifted the conversation to author Thomas Wolfe, whom he had known while living next to Max Perkins, the great Scribner's editor.

"You still writing?" he said.

I told him that I had sold a few stories to low-paying magazines.

"Good," he said, making a note. "I'm going to need

all the ammunition I can to put this across with the board."

As I left, he mentioned that our project looked more in the neighborhood of $6,000 than $3,000.

We had the winter to go through before the bankers would come up for an inspection, so we tried to get our lives in order. We cut our expenses to the bone. To keep our awareness of Caesar's coin at a fine pitch, we started assembling statements about money. The contents of *Moola Miseries* by Zeke and Marthy was filched from newspapers and anthologies:

It's called cold cash because you can't keep it long enough to get warm.

As Mark Twain said, "His money is twice tainted—t'aint yours and it t'aint mine."

You can say one thing for poverty—it sticks to you when all your friends are gone.

One of my favorites was a Chinese proverb that somebody passed along:

He that is without money might as well be buried in rice with his mouth sewed up.

On the practical side, we redoubled our efforts to use up every material thing, to throw away nothing that could be employed in a different form. Example: old, unmatched socks. They were woolen. They were warm. Phyllis piled them in a box and we used them for mittens. We tore toothpaste tubes in half to get the last dab. We tucked newspapers under threadbare sweaters to keep warm.

We used an old door for a tabletop, a World War I bayonet for a carving knife. Coat hangers were bent and cut into dozens of useful shapes, from hot-dog cookers to towel racks. We grew so accustomed to saving *everything* that we got a laugh out of each visit to the Saxtons River dump.

"See anything appetizing, Zeke?" Phyllis would say.

"There's a Maxwell muffler and a stove lid, Marthy."

The dump supplied me with metal I knew we would need when I built our second fireplace for the garage room—car bumpers, old pipe. It was astonishing what Americans threw away, even in the relatively unopulent outback. We found chairs that needed only glue or a new leg, bookcases that wanted only a well-placed screw or nail.

All of it came up the mountain in our jeep.

One Sunday, when the February icicles glinted like daggers by the kitchen window, I sat down, and listed the things I had bought the previous year that we really didn't need. I didn't include recreation items—movies, church suppers, and such—which we considered crucial to families who dwelt in the sticks.

> Silver pitcher
> Battery-powered metal detector
>   (for God's sake!)
> Post-hole digger
> Soil test kit
> New rake
> Air pump that plugged into jeep
>   spark-plug socket
> Vase (ghastly)

On and on. The list rose to more than $300 in value—and here I was, reduced to nickels and dimes again. My ire against myself rose. Many of the items were nice to own—the silver pitcher, for instance—but at this point did we *need* them? A cement-block maker bought for $25 was fine in theory, but I had never marshaled the cement, strained sand, and time needed to go with it. Besides, concrete blocks cost nineteen cents; could I manufacture them more cheaply? The post-hole digger was a good idea, but I was tearing down fences, not putting them up. The soil test kit was a gesture to agricultural gimmickery. (In three minutes Richard Bradley could tell me more about what my land would and wouldn't grow.) And the new rake was not so good as my old.

Vase, metal detector, *et al* were sheer follies. Marie Antoinette herself could not have excused them.

Finally—and worst of all—I wrote: "Pair of steel scaffold hooks. Cost: $16.75." These were designed to hook over the ridge of a steep roof so that the plank on which a worker stood was level and secure. When I first saw them in Fuller Hardware, they seemed essential. Wasn't I going to shingle my house someday? The only trouble was that my roof was not steep and I could work on it in perfect safety *without* a scaffold of any kind. Moreover, the shingles showed no signs of needing replacement.

Those scaffold hooks did it. I scribbled a sour note to myself: "Toughen up, dummy—buy for real *needs* only."

I hung the hooks prominently outside the cabin—a reproof and a warning. (Years later I gave them to a neighbor who had fixed a smashed door for me. He moved from his high-gabled house to a trailer, so the hooks never saw action, to my knowledge.)

He who buys what he doesn't need, goes the countryman's saw, *steals from himself.*

As icy winds howled a few feet from my paper-strewn table, Phyllis and I took an oath. *Buy blindly, throw away* would never again sneak into our working credo.

March arrived. The Albino Mood set in. What was

the Albino Mood? It was a subtle malaise that we had been warned about—a *feeling* that crept into mountain life between Valentine Day and Easter when the enameled whiteness of everything started to gnaw at our nerves. White snow, watery skies, pale clouds—this chill, weepy world got a nightmarish grip on our minds. It caused cabin-bound wives to burst into tears over wash buckets, and long-underweared men to howl curses (between wracking coughs) at the weather. The thrilling newness of winter was gone. We thought we couldn't stand the crackly talk of tree skeletons another twenty-four hours.

We were sick of snowflakes, thick as oatmeal, of meadows armored with ice. The *chink-a-chink* of chains was a madness. The ghostflower tone of the day made the Albino Mood as mournful as an off-tune song, heard a thousand times.

On such a gloomy afternoon, when I wasn't home, the phone rang. Susan Aldrich wanted Phyllis to send Pete down to play with Little Sue, her daughter. They were the same age, and both mothers fretted over their preschool isolation.

"Kids get so lonely this time of year," Susan said.

The Aldrich farm sprawled at the bottom of the road. Its big, handsome house sat under old maples across from red barns. Roland Aldrich, a wide-shouldered ex-machine gunner of World War II, was following a dream. He was trying to set up a Hereford breeding farm of top-quality stock. He had a bull that was worth over $20,000 and acres dotted with white-faced cattle.

The Aldriches had picnicked with us ... had given us scrap lumber for scaffolding. Pete and Little Sue were friends—and as soon as Pete heard what was being said, he began to jump.

"I want to go! I want to go!"

But there was no way. I was at Readex. Roland

61

was following an auction. The road was a desolate ribbon of mud, occasionally traversed by groaning log trucks—no place for a child of less than five.

Later that night, however, Phyllis greeted me with a smile. "This has been a great day," she said.

Richard Bradley had called, she told me. He was driving his pickup to town. Was there anything the Morrills wanted?

"I decided to let Pete walk to the Bradleys' and ride in Richard's pickup to the Aldriches'."

She stood by the gate, holding Mike in her arms. She gave Pete instructions. He was to walk straight to the Bradleys'. If a log truck passed, he was to run up the bank.

Pete took off. Every 100 feet he turned and waved—and Phyllis waved back.

At last the small red jacket disappeared around a bend. A grumble started—a log truck was coming! She shifted Mike on her hip and stared down the road. The truck thundered by, the driver nodding. At last, far beyond the bend where the road reappeared at the Bradleys', a tiny figure headed into the yard, kicking a stick with a boot.

Phyllis sank against the gate. Then she gave Mike a kiss and walked back to the cabin.

"That was what happened," she said. "And Pete's staying at the Aldriches' for supper."

"That's what happened?" I said.

"Yes."

"All?"

She stared at me. "Don't you see? He went by himself. He kept waving and looking back—but he went."

"He must have looked cute."

Her eyes glistened. "He looked brave and beautiful. And so small. He'll never look that way again on the road. He passed by something—don't you see?"

I smiled as she blew her nose. It *had* been a great day.

Feather did nothing to ease our friendship with the Aldriches. He growled when Roland's tractor came up the mountain. He tolerated Little Sue if she came to play with Pete, but kept his distance.

One April morning, when pale green was showing on the birches and the sky shone like moist sapphire, he disgraced us. He chewed himself loose and caught our jeep just as we reached the farm. Roland's prize boxer, rippling with muscle, came out to defend his territory.

Feather met his attack head on.

It was a snarling brawl. Fur and blood flew. Three-legged Feather upended the boxer and slashed his shoulder. Roland and I finally tore them apart. But the next day the prize boxer died in his sleep, while Feather, with purple tongue flapping happily, was circling below a treed raccoon.

It was really a disaster. I felt obligated to pay for Roland's dog. But he wouldn't take the money.

"The boxer must have had a bad heart anyhow," he said. "Say, that maverick of yours is some scrapper."

"He's trouble from the word go."

Toward the end of the month, Feather disappeared. We called in the woods, down the road.

"He's off on a toot," I said. "He'll show up."

But he didn't. Days passed. I began asking trappers downtown to visit their traps.

Then Richard Bradley drew me aside and said hesitantly, "I didn't want to speak out—for the boy's sake. . . ."

"Feather's dead?" I guessed.

He nodded.

"How?"

"He got shot."

I felt my neck grow warm. "Who shot him?"

He wouldn't tell me. For the first and only time I had a surge of resentment against this soft-spoken old farmer.

"Why not tell me?"

"It would just make feeling on the hill," he explained miserably, "like a that."

I said that shooting a man's dog was a goddamn mean thing, and he agreed. I said that a guy who would shoot a man's dog and not come and tell him about it was a lousy sonofabitch, and he agreed.

He also agreed to my other expressions of outrage. But he wouldn't tell me who pulled the trigger.

I didn't tell Pete the truth. I made up a story about how Feather was off chasing a tough old wildcat to Canada, a prolonged adventure. For quite a while I was miffed at Richard Bradley, but gradually I realized that he had acted prudently. I *thought* I knew who had done the killing—a guy from Massachusetts who had once lived on the mountain and often hunted there. But it could have been someone else. Perhaps Feather charged him. Perhaps Feather had been attacking sheep or deer, a capital offense.

In any case, Richard knew that I was in no condition to face the executioner.

How we loved Feather!

As spring of 1952 came on, we got ready for the bankers' visit. I hauled all our junk behind bushes. I cleared fallen branches from the yard. I scythed the hay and slapped a coat of cheap green paint on our outside table.

Phyllis scrubbed our floors and windows.

They came—grave, courteous men in business suits.

Z Persons whispered to me. "Talk it up. Show 'em all those hot ideas."

I waxed eloquent. I took wings and soared. Here in this sylvan paradise we would construct an Elysian postwar life—a return to the time-tried American ethic of hard work, stern self-restraint, and happy achievement. This was no fly-by-night operation, no, sir. We had been tested in the blizzard bowl, and we still intended to make rural Vermont our Home Sweet Home.

In the back of my skull, I heard *The Stars and Stripes Forever* blowing faintly.

Next day Z Persons called again. "Those fellows told me I get them in the damnedest spread eagles."

They granted us a mortgage for up to $6,000.

That same afternoon I sold a story to *Adventure* magazine for $200. We did a dance in the living room. Ah, rose-crowned children of destiny, beloved of the gods! We went out to the Highlands Restaurant for supper and tried to look casual amid all the station wagon travelers with their firsthand clothes.

The idea was to make every dollar do as much work as it could. We shopped around and discovered that we could buy a precut building from Maine, 20 by 34 feet, including windows and doors, for $2,275. It was a shell only, but a gloriously large one. One end of it would be a two car garage; the other, a large room with fireplace and bath.

"We'll throw it up parallel to the cabin," I said, "then connect the two buildings with a breezeway."

"Out *there*?" Phyllis asked, pointing incredulously.

The site was thick with trees, several a foot and a half thick. Worse, it sloped sharply from the northeast corner. And it looked ledgy.

I snapped my fingers. "Cinch."

We ordered the building. I went to work with my ax. The first tree doubled back unexpectedly and bounced off the cabin, ripping some shingles. The next two leaned against other trees and wouldn't drop.

"How's it going, Mr. Cinch?" Phyllis called through the kitchen window.

All that summer, I worked nights and weekends—and things never got better. I cut and stacked the heavy timber. When I started the foundation ditch, my pick chimed against quartz and feldspar at a dozen different levels. The stumps seemed to have a death grip on the stone. Mocking rains came—and came and came. I sloshed around in my Merchant Marine boots, growling.

One late afternoon, coming home from Readex, I stopped behind a stalled log truck. Two men, stripped to the waist, with biceps muscles like turnips, were bent over the motor.

One said, "*Hold* the wire, you dumb skunk-fucker."

The other said, "I ain't squeezing a tit, ass-face."

They exchanged other affabilities, increasing in amperage, until the motor roared to life. Then they nodded in friendly fashion and drove on.

Continuing home, I reflected on the power of profanity. Schools taught that it indicated a destitution of language—true much of the time. But sometimes it represented an enrichment. In the Vermont countryside it distinctly safety-valved a tough work day and therefore had its worth.

Having been to sea, I came adequately armed with cuss words, and they had always stood me in good stead. I knew that a fluorescent fixture went into an off-level ceiling more easily if I called it a sonofabitch at least three times. Also, if I stared at a quivering, hammer-smashed thumb and said, "Holy, jumped-up, hell-hopping Christ!" the pain was somehow softened.

In the lip-artillery department, however, I had not been prepared for the explosive originality of the

Vermont woodsmen. These sinewy young men worked all day with chain saws and log pikes. Scratched by brambles, bitten by flies, they developed their own verbal defenses.

I drove on, thinking. In Chester I had gotten to know a logger who sometimes worked as a diner cook. He was also a heavyweight boxer and would occasionally go to New York to fight in boxing clubs. One day I had met him outside Readex, with the right hand in bandage and splint.

"What happened?" I asked.

"Horse stepped on my goddamn foot," he said.

He was limping, I noticed. But the hand?

"Well, when that mare-fucking glue pot stomped me, I aimed a KO punch right at his jaw."

I waited.

"Connected on the button, by Jesus," he said.

"Yeah?"

"You know, my fist broke in four places? And that hoss didn't even blink, that sonbitch of a ———" He bent double, filling the air with imprecations. The birch leaves curled. The earth quivered. All horsedom choked in sulfur.

He came to a sputtering finish. "And now I'm washed up. Can't hit nothing ever again—son of a triple bitch!"

Around Saxtons River I had recorded some colorful talk. It was lusty rather than gooey. I heard one hapless guy called "a rancid, apple-wormed bastard"; and another, "about as significant as a fart in a Canada blizzard." One bulldozer operator had told me that a competitor's "bullshit runs six tons to a barrel." And somebody else had commented that Rutland Fair was "jam-packed as a Guernsey's ass in fly season."

I turned up our mountain, shifting into four-wheel drive. The sky glowed like fire opal. Ahead of me was an hour of hard-scrabble exercise on the damned site. Maybe I needed a new cuss phrase to lubricate my toil—a real ripper.

When we had started our Vermont venture, I had settled on the relatively mild "bitch-bastard!" It had a nice syllabic rhythm, a one-two effect. And it could roll off my tongue without thought. Furthermore, muttered low, I could get away with it in ordinary company, for it had no scatological overtones.

I experimented, barking a few foul oaths at the windshield. But they didn't do anything for me. There was a special blasphemy for loggers, for hunters—maybe for cabin builders.

Then I thought: *Why not give up the whole business, just to see if you can?*

I arrived home and began to work. Things went badly, as usual. My shovel hit ledge.

"Oh, my!" I said.

Phyllis, getting supper, looked out the screen door.

A moment later my ax went through a root that was rotten, clanged against rock, and flew out of my hands.

"Zounds and fudge," I said.

Phyllis, holding a dish of potatoes, peered through the window. She started to say something, but turned away.

A few moments after that an extraordinary thing happened. I swung a sledgehammer against a large stone. Rock fragments spat sideways into some brush. Instantly hornets streamed out—a nest of them! I leaped from the shallow ditch, but one foot skidded back. My floppy pant leg slid over the handle of my ax, which was standing upright. I lost my balance and tumbled backward into the ditch, lifting the ax handle with my pant leg so that it broke a pitcher of water sitting on the edge. Water and glass fell on my stomach.

"BITCH-BASTARD!"

Phyllis served the vegetables and poured coffee. "I knew you were all right," she said, "as soon as you stopped talking Russian."

Yard by yard, the foundation rectangle took shape. The footing ditch roller coasted up and down with the ledge, so I had to build dikes on separate levels there. This was in order that the concrete blocks, eight inches in height, could be laid evenly. The completed foundation, I could see, would run from a two-block depth in one corner to nine blocks at the opposite end. I began mixing concrete in my old sleigh body. Before dawn and after supper, I churned away. I dumped each mess in the footing. It plopped, jiggled, and sat there—an insignificant gray dot. Mixing for this job was a lot slower than mixing for a chimney.

"If I go on like this," I said, "some passing circus will nab me for the Human Skeleton."

We calculated carefully, then ordered a truckload of concrete from Brattleboro. I reinforced our bridge with stone to carry the great weight. The truck snorted up our road like a mastodon, tearing branches out of the trees. The concrete gushed down the chute. We directed it into the diked footing with shovels and hoes. Phyllis, after an earlier false alarm, was pregnant again, but I couldn't keep her out of the action. Pete pushed with a stick.

For the next month every spare minute was consumed laying blocks. It rained steadily. At last the foundation was finished—a fortlike rectangle with stumps jutting up inside. I hired Al Williams again.

The precut building arrived from Maine. We had to knock down our wagon-wheel gate to let the massive trailer truck in. We piled rafter sections, siding units, and bundles of shingles beside the footing.

69

Could we get the thing up? Suddenly came a succession of yellow days—skies blue as larkspur. Al Williams and I hammered away. Birds chattered. May scents pushed through the lush hills. The white skeleton of two-by-fours arose to the tuneful *plink-plank-plunk* of sixpenny nails slamming home, while we joked and sang.

After the roof was on, we dug the breezeway foundation. We hauled stone for a new chimney. Money dribbled, flowed, and gushed away.

"Everything you do in the construction business costs exactly double your estimates."

"That's it!" said Phyllis. "You've formed a law—Morrill's Law."

I swallowed bleakly. Fame at last.

We sped past my original $3,000 projection, hit $4,000 without breaking stride, and closed in on $5,000. I walked around with figures jumping in my head.

In nearby Gageville I found a rugged young truck driver who was tearing apart several old CCC camp barracks.

"Want to sell some lumber?"

He hoisted his foot on my bumper. "Might."

"Two-by-fours, two-by-sixes, flooring?"

"Might."

"I'm trying to build—"

"So am I."

He was converting one building into a home and cannibalizing out of the others. He took me through rooms sheathed in U.S. Government plywood.

"Your work looks better than mine," I said.

"I'm just a hacker."

He sold me lumber at less than half price. We piled it into the trailer. He handed me a can of beer and knocked sawdust from his hair.

"You know," he said, "all of us guys building homes around these hills—we're going to make it.

Don't matter whether we're half broke or pooped out. This country will support a man. Only requirement is that you bust your ass."

I scrounged around plumbing warehouses in Bellows Falls, hunting fixtures for the new bathroom. I found a dusty tub on which a carpenter had dropped his hammer, marring it with a small spider mark.

"Forty bucks?" I offered.

"A deal," said the plumber. "Say, you the guy building on Hartley Hill?"

"Trying to."

"Well, hang in there. Country needs young fellas. You'll have something—after you git four or five hernias putting it up."

I picked up a toilet bowl and sink at a Sears sale, and a farmer at Fuller Hardware snorted. "Hope they don't chip on you—mine did." I found glass towel racks at a used furniture shop for fifty cents, and a door at the dump for nothing.

We built the breezeway and kitchen extension rapidly. One day Albert Boni took me down cellar at Readex. He waved at a pile of junk and timbers.

"Let's get rid of that," he said.

Free stuff! I hauled out two-by-fours and plywood studded with nails. There were a couple of dozen cinder blocks, and—best of all—a 10-by-10 inch beam that would make a fine mantel for our new fireplace.

"If we keep on getting windfalls," I said, "maybe we can stay within the budget."

"What budget?" said Phyllis. "The last one was on the back of an envelope. It passed to the Great Beyond weeks ago."

"Well, let's pretend we're working on a strict financial blueprint. . . ."

She spread ten fingers four times. "Figure a baby in forty days."

I bit the nail with new economies, even giving up a

71

fifteen-cent cigar on Sundays. But, after paying for a fuel tank, power saw, chimney tile, electric drill, floor stain, brushes, and more knotty-pine paneling, I began to look at the checkbook with alarm. Adding the costs of wiring, Al Williams's wages, and paint, I found we were passing our $6,000 limit.

"Believe it or not, it will take seven hundred more dollars to get this whole thing over the goal line."

We blinked at the figures. They glared back, cold and correct.

"Well, let's take a chance," I said. "I'll sell a couple of stories and bail us out."

"Easy, Zeke . . . ," said Phyllis.

I ordered everything we needed to wind up the job—gravel, cement, ceiling panels, bulldozer time, I said farewell to Al Williams, with regret. Using the splintery lumber of packing crates from Readex, I built myself an 8-by-8-foot room in the garage, larger and more solid than my outhouse office. I covered the walls with foil insulation that came from waterproof boxes at Readex. I ran wires from the cabin to a timer and hooked the timer to an electrically powered milk-house heater.

For the first time, I owned a heated room in which to write. Sternly I pushed aside all thoughts of the house, except an occasional thrill of anxiety that we now had a debt of $700, due in thirty days—and no funds to meet it.

I set the timer for 3:00 A.M. At 5:00 I stumbled out to the warm cubicle. The heater whirred. Franklin D. Roosevelt meowed. I dug into my notes, searching for a salable idea.

By this time I had sold a number of sea stories, mostly to such magazines as *Argosy* and *Adventure*. If I could write one or two for a total of $600, we might squeak by.

Finally I wrote the story of a Brooklyn rabbi in the

South Pacific. I tried to put in what I could remember of that lustrous wartime ocean where ordinary things appeared in new, Brobdingnagian perspective—mile-long clouds rimmed with taffy-colored sunlight, gulls dipped in silver. I tried to recapture the tragic twilights, crumbling in mauve and gold. And I threw in terror when the Oriental night stepped over the horizon, a tuxedoed jinni with a splendid vest of stars.

The *Saturday Evening Post* bought the story for $1,000.

My steam up, I wrote another about a Seabee welder and his cranky commander, caught in a Japanese air raid on New Britain. The *Post* took it for $1,250.

What went on here? I was stunned. We paid off our debt and jumped back in the construction business. (I kept writing in spare moments, of course, but I wasn't to sell another word to the *Post* for five years.)

"That was close," said Phyllis.

Made It to Here

WE CALLED the new structure the "ell." The word had a baronial overtone, as if we had attached a lavish wing to a castle. I nailed up knotty-pine walls and built a closet. The only task left was to put in a fireplace on the western end, next to the picture window, but that could wait.

"I'm installing the floor furnace so it blows both ways—into the room and the garage," I said. "Just think, a heated garage."

"Just think, a heated room," said Phyllis.

The family overflowed into the new section, like a circus fat lady bursting her corset. Everything cascaded in—books, tools, chinaware, toys, suitcases, clothes. . . . Phyllis unloaded diapers and baby bottles. Where did it all come from?

"We're getting like everybody else—locked into the system," I said.

Our cabin was becoming a house. And we were no longer a dewy-eyed couple with a baby. We were a slightly worn mother and father with two kids and another soon to arrive. Phyllis and I looked around us: *So this is growing up!* Pete, nearly six, was a miniature workman—a lifter of grocery bags and a nailer of nails. Mike, too, was already a hauler of firewood in his little red wagon.

Yes, we were like the rest of the world after all—a young family becoming not-so-young.

"I'm not too keen about the way time is flying," said Phyllis.

I took her on a house tour to show what we had accomplished. The living room glowed with maple furniture and a home-built oaken record player. The wall above the fireplace was crisscrossed with oiled swords and machetes, brought from Central America and the Orient. The bedroom bunks were finished, with storage doors underneath that swung on Colonial-style H and L hinges. Mike's crib was backed against my bookcases outside our room.

In the attic, which we used as a storeroom-playroom, Pete had hung up bright maritime signal flags from some forgotten ship I had sailed. Our lone trunk was open, and he and Mike had been rummaging amid old treasures—pictures, letters, a broken set of ivory chopsticks. . . . I picked up a grass skirt I had brought from the Pacific during the war.

"Remember this—for a slim, young thing?" I said.

Phyllis snatched it. "Don't get smart. I could still put it on."

She did a brief hula, holding it to her bulging waist, then tossed it down.

"The Last Fertility Dance," she said.

The kitchen had new shamrock-colored linoleum sporting yellow designs of our own making. The old stove had a scrap-wood cabinet underneath and a rock maple cutting board alongside. Phyllis's red curtains and potted geraniums twinkled in the sun.

"This is one cheery joint," I said.

"It would be cheerier if we could buy or steal a bed for the ell," she said.

"Fate will provide."

And, sure enough, my sister jettisoned a double bed from her swanky new trailer in New Hampshire. We wrestled it into the ell and placed it so that a guest could go to sleep with starlight from the picture window brushing his eyelids.

The garage end of the ell filled up with alarming speed. Besides the corner taken for my packing-crate office, space was preempted by a long tool bench, a freezer, some steel lockers (bought for a song from a shut-down business), and a mountain of firewood. Pretty soon there was no room for a car.

"So what's new about a jeep staying out?" I said. "It will survive the winters—thanks to our superior American technology."

"I hope it starts—thanks to the same," said Phyllis.

Pleased as we were with the ell, nobody wanted to move there permanently. Phyllis and I were used to our side-by-side bunks with their reading lights. Pete liked his own room with picture-covered walls. And Mike was too young to be marooned on the other side of the breezeway, although it would have been nice to convert his small sleeping space back to a library.

The ell, we soon realized, was extra territory to be used as a playroom, a guest chamber, a storage bin, or an escape hatch when anyone wanted to be alone. Noting its sunny southern windows, Phyllis placed our baby basket there to await its new occupant—for future use during daylight hours.

We even considered eating out there. There was plenty of space for a dining table, and at the moment we were squeezed around three sides of a counter in the kitchen. But the idea died.

"I can see us lugging food back and forth on the breezeway at twenty below," said Phyllis. "No dice."

"That's the way they did it on Southern plantations," I protested. "Old Mammy toting the platter."

"Smiling and shuffling?"

"Working happy for her folks, same as you."

"Well, we'll stick to the comfy ol' New England nook by the stove. Like a that."

The ell (the garage half, that is) helped Pete and Mike grow up even faster. Time and again, I would hear them out there working with hammers and saws. Pete made wooden swords and a primitive crossbow. He cut boards into pieces for Mike to pound together and call boats.

Some Saturdays when Mike was taking his nap, Pete would hang around my office door and talk. Usually, I would be trying to write. A typical conversation (which I scribbled in my notebook) went like this:

"Dad, do you know how you could teach a dog to talk?"

"No."

"Well, you could make him say 'bow' and leave off the 'wow'—and that's the front of a ship."

"That right?"

"Then you could surprise him and he'd say 'wow!' So that would be 'Bowwow.' "

"Uh huh."

"I wish our cats could talk."

"Hey kid, I've got to type."

"Is that how you make money?"

"I try."

"If a man offered you fifty thousand million dollars for a peanut, would you take it?"

Fortunately, cold weather isolated me in my heated niche much of the time. It was hard enough to concentrate on slick, magazine fantasy without wandering into Pete's child world, alluring as it was. Unless it rained, the boys usually spent their hours outside playing with the cats or pulling their wagons. So story writing inched on.

Phyllis was changing. Blue eyes graver, prettier. I found her with uplifted arm, cutting her hair in front of a mirror. *Snip*—some curls fell off. She handed them to me.

"See—a gray hair."

The hair was soft and sweet smelling in my palm. Unmistakably, there was a silvery thread amid the brown. I held it up to the light.

"A ribbon of honor," I said.

She plucked it back. "It isn't all that peachy."

She dropped it into the wastebasket.

Where Are We Headed?

IT WAS deep fall again, 1952. A parchment of hills tinted everything brown and tan. Dead leaves crackled under the heel. I knew we had lucked through, and I wanted to be cautious, but one night I saw Phyllis's hands on the bedcover as she slept.

Her fingers were cracked and red from washing clothes. Our $15 washing machine was just a shade better than pounding the wash in a brook with a canoe paddle; she did a lot of wringing by hand.

I'm going to get an automatic washer.

The bank account said no. The jeep had just had a clutch job, and—for the first time—I had bought an insurance policy. The new baby was only days away.

"That will be three hundred and twenty-five dollars—plus installation charges," said the man in Bellows Falls.

No, thanks.

"Your water is gravity feed? You can't have an automatic washer—not enough pressure," said the man in Springfield.

Gracias.

79

"Hell," said the Chester guy, "them automatics are one hundred percent trouble. I got a wringer-type just the ticket—one hundred and eighty-five dollars."

Nyet.

But the news was out—the Morrills were looking for a washing machine. The Saturday I returned home from taking Phyllis to the hospital, Hoppy Dodge was waiting in a pickup.

"Hear you're in the market," he said.

Hoppy was Roland Aldrich's hired man. He was a short, bouncy Vermonter with brawny arms and eyes that crinkled. He cocked his cap and spat.

"How's the new baby?"

I said we didn't have one yet.

"Go give Phyllis a few Indian whoops through the window. That will start her."

Hoppy was a jack-of-all-trades. He could grin. On the abandoned Kimball Road, he had nailed an arrow-shaped sign: COWS—TURN HERE. Every day Roland's cows did just that, swinging off to their accustomed pasture by themselves, and Hoppy swore the cows could read.

"Washing machine's a serious proposition," he said.

"Don't I know it, Hop. I can't spend over one hundred dollars."

He walked around. He examined our water pressure and pooh-poohed the man who said we couldn't have an automatic. We would have to dig a dry well for it, though.

"If you run detergent into your septic tank, you'll wreck the action—kill all the bacteria."

"How about my cash limit—one hundred bucks?"

"Git digging the dry well. I'll come up with something."

I dug a four-foot well and lined it with loose stones. I bent flat some heavy steel shoes from old wagon wheels and laid them across the well, edge up, to support a sheet-metal cover.

Hoppy examined it. "Hell, I wouldn't object to having a tea party in there. Rinso-Brite will love it."

He helped me run a soil pipe from the kitchen.

"We have everything but the washing machine," I said.

"Pray."

The phone rang. The doctor said, "Were you figuring on a girl?"

All I wanted to know was if Phyllis was okay.

"Well, you've got another boy—and your wife's fine."

In the hospital Phyllis and I groped for a middle name to the thin-faced little squaller she held at her breast. She had already decided to call him Christopher.

"I suggest Columbus," I said.

She lifted her eyes to the ceiling. "That does it, God. No middle name."

We let it ride at "Christopher Morrill."

Hoppy drove onto the Flat, a white Bendix roped in his pickup. "Morrisons are getting a new one. There's plenty of mileage in this here button-popper yet."

We installed it next to our $20 Frigidaire and stared at suds churning in the circular window.

"She's better than TV," said Hoppy. "You can make any kind of picture you want on that screen."

The total cost was $75.

That night Pete and I polished the washer until it glittered. I painted over a scratch. In the morning I took him with me to Readex (Mike was in Connecticut with his grandmother), and we left the plant early to bring Phyllis home.

Pete glanced dutifully at his new brother, but he

81

kept bouncing up and down behind Phyllis's seat. "Wait till you see what we got! Wait till you see!"

It was a moment not to forget. Phyllis tucked Christopher into his basket at the foot of her bunk and walked slowly to the kitchen.

"Hold your hands over her eyes, Dad."

We positioned her in front of the jewellike machine. Pete turned the chromium dial. The motor whirred.

"Oh!"

She stared at it. Then she wheeled around, face in her fists.

"Don't look at me."

The night dissolved in wet cheeks and laughter. We drank hot chocolate. We watched in awe while the wondrous Bendix hummed through its full cycle.

Snow billowed in, followed by bitter cold. One night, when the moon made a wickery radiance through the trees, Phyllis sat up in her bunk.

"I can't seem to breathe," she said.

I turned on the light. Her face was flushed.

"My throat feels tight—that's funny."

I brought her some water, our sparkling remedy-for-all-ills that flowed from the deeps of the mountain.

"Just small sips," I said.

She tried to drink, but fell back gasping. I called Doc Griffith in Chester, who had delivered Christopher.

"Be right over," he said. "Meet me at the bottom of the hill with your jeep."

I left Phyllis propped in a chair by the fireplace, her brown curls damp on her forehead. Pete, Mike, and Baby Chris slept in their warm sheets.

"Keep inhaling as deep as you can," I told her.

The snow squeaked underfoot. It was 18 below. My

breath made a ragged smoke in the moonlight. For a miracle, the jeep roared to life at the first starter-kick, and I started down the frozen road.

A century passed. My boots kicked ice chunks at the bottom of the hill. The Aldrich farm loomed, dark and silent.

Phyllis is strong. She's breathing okay.

At last Doc's headlights jiggled up the road. His bulky shoulders settled into the jeep seat. He tucked his bag between his knees, and I rammed the jeep into four-wheel drive.

It was a ride. The motor screamed. Barbed wire raced past, dipping in and out of drifts like knotted string.

The second we arrived, Doc ran for the house. Even before he reached the door, he began fumbling in his bag.

Phyllis was twisted sideways in the chair, half conscious. Doc filled his hypodermic and jammed the needle into her arm. Then he held her head back so that her rasping breath came easier.

She opened her eyes—and grinned.

Afterward, I made coffee. I dumped some empty cereal cartons onto the fire coals and tossed in a birch log. Doc explained that this was just a little penicillin reaction, that's all. They had given her a few shots at the hospital to halt an infection after the baby was born.

"From now on don't let anyone use penicillin on her. She reacts like a bombshell."

Within fifteen minutes, Phyllis's swollen face began to subside. Doc stayed, telling stories of his emergency calls in far-flung farmhouses.

"You're pretty much out in the sticks right here," he said. "Desert from the Foreign Legion?"

Long after taking him back to his car, I sat by

Phyllis's bunk. When she fell asleep, I threw on my old sailor's jacket and stepped outside again.

The world was a frozen wedding cake. Cracked, white clouds towered up, with an egg-colored moon leaking through. I followed some ski tracks to the Knoll. The valley lay like an ocean of silver, and I could feel icy air prickling the inside of my nose.

I asked myself the question posed by all young men trying to build lives of their own: *What in the world am I doing in this place?*

It was time to think about this. Three and a half years had slipped by. . . .

Originally we had simply fled from a vague fear of being trapped in suburbia. Somewhere in the back of our heads had flickered the idea that Americans ought to return to the land. Perhaps this was a romantic attachment to an idyllic past that had never really existed. But all I had to do was go to a city and fill my lungs with exhaust fumes and my ears with clangor to be convinced that I was right.

"We're hooked on stars and distance," Phyllis had said.

Still, was it right to inflict cold, loneliness—and now danger—on a burgeoning family?

I paced around the marble-packed snow. A meteor flared and fell. Well, we were fumbling for a richer life. That was a goal worth a struggle. But was the cost getting too high? And who knew the obstacles ahead before we could nail down this property way out here where good-paying jobs didn't exist?

Round and round went my thoughts. I walked back to the house. Phyllis stirred under her blankets. I draped an overcoat over her feet, and she woke up.

"Did you check Christopher?"

"He's okay."

"Exciting night, Zeke."

"How do you feel, babe?"

She squeezed my hand. "I wouldn't trade the life up here for any other. We've got to finish this place. We'll keep it forever."

Warm weather drifted in, making everything wet. Then, without warning, a blizzard struck. Blinding snow locked us in for two days. When the sun came out, it was the most we could do to dig a narrow path to where the road was buried. Pete, red-faced and rugged, worked with a small wooden shovel.

He had grown bright and mountainwise since his epic walk down the road. Now he was ready for early school. His mind danced with ideas.

"Pretend we're miners digging silver," he said.

Sunlight spanked on daisy drifts. We shoveled in white-and-blue stillness.

"Maybe we'll find emeralds here," I said, "or sapphires and rubies."

"Yeah!"

By the time we finished, castles with jeweled spires towered on the Knoll. Alabaster forts frowned on Big Baldy.

"It's just like real," said Pete, looking around in wonder.

Back at the house, he broke off an icicle. He declared it a diamond, and Phyllis gravely placed it in the refrigerator.

The next morning we heard a loud grumble and saw smoke puffing behind a drift. Then a mountain of snow rose up by our gate, smoking and crumbling.

"Our mine is blowing up!" cried Pete.

Soon a tiger-yellow bulldozer burst through, destroying our belief in a magic hand at work. A town driver, wrapped to the nose in a red scarf, pushed bladeful after bladeful of snow in a mighty pile.

"There's our fort, Pete."

We rushed out with shovels. The snow pile was sixteen feet high and at least forty feet square. It was packed hard in ledges at various levels and had hollow areas inside.

We sculpted a snow fort such as the world has never seen. It had ramps and passageways, battlements and gates. I planted a rag-towel flag on its highest tower.

Of course, it was never attacked—not even by a snowball. Few people ever saw it. But Pete, walking the escarpment with a lathe sword, fended off spectral enemies for hours each day. When I came home from work, my headlights would find him—a solitary Davy Crockett pointing a log cannon at me.

As long as the fort lasted, he and I acted out dramas there. After supper, canyon colors deepened. One star shone in the Knoll's naked maple, bright as a teardrop. We would grapple with phantom knights and pirates. Swords flashing, we would race up snow ramps, leap over battlements, and slay our enemies in windrows.

For an hour or so, our cries would prick the vast stillness. The action always ended with a tribe of phantom Indians capturing the fort. Prisoners now, our only hope was escape by our sled, which, fortunately, we had planted on the Knoll, facing downhill.

"Sneak toward the Knoll, Dad," Pete whispered.

Arguing with the grim, unseen Indians, we eased toward freedom. At last I belly whopped onto the sled, Pete pushed us off and leaped onto my back, and we zoomed down the slope, howling taunts at our pursuers. The run was laced with ice. *Ka-whamp*, a bump at the bottom flung us off like rag dolls. Swirling wildly, we wound up in tangles, our wrists and cheeks stinging with snow.

It was a new game each night until the thaw.

Winter wouldn't let go. Wet snow and sodden clouds wrapped the mountain in flannel. A blurt of sunshine came through now and then; but before we could feel its warmth on our cheeks, it vanished.

"We're going to the Fathers and Sons Banquet in three days," Pete told me. "You said."

"Oh, that's right."

"Don't forget—*you said.*"

How could I forget? The Fathers and Sons Banquet was an event of the year, and every kid in Saxtons River kept reminding his Old Man about it. Held in the Federated Church basement, this soiree featured talks, movies, and steaming heaps of food. For weeks beforehand, the kid world buzzed with rumors about what dish was to be served, what cartoon shown.

The day arrived, hand in hand with an unexpected ice storm. Darkness drifted down early. Driving home from Chester, I cursed the jeep's coughing and sputtering. By the time I reached O'Connor's Garage, the motor seemed to be hitting on two cylinders.

"Looks like a blown gasket," said Bob. "Better leave her here."

I phoned Phyllis. "Tell Pete sorry. We can't make the banquet."

"Oh, dear."

Behind her I heard an agonized voice cry, "What's the matter?"

"Bob can't fix the jeep till tomorrow," I said. "I'll hook a ride up the hill with Bradley."

"Oh, dear, Pete has been polishing his shoes all afternoon, and he'll be so disa—"

A wail arose. "WE CAN'T GO TO THE BANQUET?"

I peered across the phone at the frozen street ... at vapor rising from the post office. People slapped their mittens together and blew balloons of frost. It was madness to try to drive up our mountain.

"I'll see if I can make it," I said.

I coaxed the jeep out of the garage. Even going up the slight rise by Tenney's Lumber Mill, I had to shift to second gear. When I reached the Dows' culvert where the road pitched upward, the car nearly stalled, but I jammed her into four-wheel drive, low range and low gear. I pushed the gas to the floor.

Straining, belching smoke, the engine inched uphill. Walls of plowed snow crept by. I parked at our gate, pointing down.

"It's crazy to go out tonight," I told Phyllis. "I'll never get started after the banquet."

Pete was dressed in his best clothes, hair slicked down, shoes gleaming. "Please, Dad, PLEASE. We can. . . ." He choked and ran to his room.

"He's been on his knees by the window," said Phyllis, "*praying*."

We had to push the jeep to get started. Phyllis, in apron and overcoat, strained against a fender. We rolled onto crackling ice. Pete and I jumped in. Phyllis waved. It took nearly a quarter of a mile for the engine to kick to life.

I parked on a steep incline across from the firehouse. All through the banquet, as Pete chattered and laughed with friends, I thought of the two-mile hike home—probably carrying a sleepy kid the last 400 yards.

But afterward the jeep rolled down, coughed, and began to pulsate feebly. We chugged up our road, with even the heater mercifully blowing.

"See?" said Pete.

The next morning I was too weary to pull out at five to write. I lay groggily awake, staring at an icicle silhouette outside the window. Something bothered me. I had actually enjoyed the banquet. I had talked to men I scarcely knew—work-worn guys like myself, who had chopped time out of heavy schedules to set up the arrangements. What bothered me was the thought that I was somehow retreating from life, isolating myself and family from the normal rush of things. Shouldn't we be down there some of the time—serving on committees, helping with these functions?

I stirred around uneasily until breakfast time. Pete had shown an eagerness—almost a *desperation*—to mix with people.

I stood at the mirror shaving. I mulled and considered. But how could I move into village affairs and get my job done up here too? *And* write? I couldn't—that was all.

The hell with it.

I rolled the jeep to O'Connor's and hitched a ride to Readex in a milk truck.

How Do You Do, Saxtons River

MAY AT LAST. One chill morning a bridal gauze of snow lay on the ruts; the next, Phyllis was spreading rugs in the hot sun. The sky turned China blue. Tootling little birds rowed through air thick with pollen. But for some reason, we felt logy and uninspired.

"Something's haywire this spring," I said.

"I know," said Phyllis. "I feel it too."

We smoked and talked and didn't arrive at much. Then Christopher began to cry and she went in to change him. We were tired or bored—or something. There were still jobs galore to keep us busy, but we were just walking through them.

"Where's the zing?" asked Phyllis.

Could we be weary of our experiment so soon? I dismissed the thought with alarm.

That very day a new facet turned our way. A white-haired man appeared on the Knoll, carrying what looked like a wooden shoebox. "Thompson," he said, shaking hands.

Mr. Thompson was a bee hunter. He wanted permission to work on our land. "I think there's a swarm somewhere below your woods," he said.

We watched, fascinated. Mr. Thompson smeared a sugary concoction on a sliding drawer of the box. He set the box in the midst of some clover and moved away from it. About fifteen minutes later, a honeybee landed on the drawer.

"Ah," he said.

He closed the drawer, trapping the bee, which went on gathering the sweet food underneath a low screen. He took a soft piece of orange chalk and, through the screen, marked the bee on his furry back. Then he opened the drawer again. After a while the bee flew off, circled the box, then headed below our woods.

"He'll bring others from the swarm, I hope," Mr. Thompson said.

We learned that, back home, the bee would do a little dance for his fellow bees. The angle of his body and the swiftness of his movements would show the direction of the food.

Sure enough, the bees started arriving. After a while, the chalked one reappeared.

"Here's our friend. Now we know that it's his swarm we're getting."

The old bee hunter chalked a new one. "Now we'll time how long it takes this chalked one to get to his colony and back here," said Mr. Thompson. "Then we can figure approximately how far away the colony is."

Half an hour later he decided that the bees were concentrated about a mile away. He began moving the box in the direction of the bees' flight every fifteen minutes.

"You have to move in a straight line with them," he said, "or they'll lose the box. And you've got to give them plenty of time to get used to each new position."

Bee hunting, I observed, could consume a lot of time.

He laughed. "Oh, yes. I won't find this hive before dark, but I'll get a line on it for the future. Probably it's in a hollow tree."

Was the reward worth the effort?

He looked at me. "You ever tasted wild honey?"

Besides, wasn't it a corking good day? How could you use up an afternoon better?

Mr. Thompson worked on, and finally vanished in the woods. I never learned whether he found the bees. But he got me thinking.

"I want some bees," I said.

I talked with Guy Austin downtown, a master beekeeper who also happened to be a barber. Gray-haired, heavyset, outspoken, Guy was an unclassifiable mixture of talents. At sixty-five, he ran a woodworking shop in back of his house—and had the reputation of being able to fix almost anything.

"Kids all grown up," he said, "so I fiddle around with this and that to keep busy, hah."

He was still the only barber in town, and he still charged only fifty cents a haircut. His customers sat on a piano stool amid wood shavings while he snipped away. He brushed the cuttings off their shoulders with a hawk's wing.

"How do you keep the bees from stinging you, Guy?"

"Hah. Now and then every beekeeper gets nipped. But a good sting just charges up the system—like electricity."

Guy agreed to sell me one of his eight hives of bees. He told me what to get—gloves, a screened mask, a smoker.

Smoker?

"It's a can with a spout and bellows. You build a little fire inside and puff smoke at the bees. It's supposed to calm them when they're feeling mean—hah."

I cleared a forest area. On a sunny Memorial Day I moved the buzzing hive in. Suddenly little bulletlike objects zoomed past my eyes. *Three angry bees were inside my mask.*

I dropped the hive. "Bitch-bastard."

Frantically I struck at the bees through the mask. But all three nailed me, one on the tip of the nose. I fled.

Phyllis and Pete, watching from a distance, doubled over.

It was three hours before I dared return to right the hive. Again the bees poured out in rage. I pumped the smoker at them, but no smoke emerged. I had neglected to relight the paper inside.

Routed again, I tightened my bee suit, retucked my double layer of pants into my double layer of socks. I circled the hive, forty feet away.

"Show confidence," shouted Phyllis. "They can't do this to you."

Four bee bites later, the hive was in position. Phyllis daubed Arm & Hammer Baking Soda on my swollen nose.

"The zing is back," she said.

Word of the Great Bee Venture got out. I picked up some guffaws downtown. Hoppy Dodge observed that a good bee trainer could make his bees loop the loop on command.

He said, "I knew a man who'd just hold out a peanut butter saandwich and his bees would bomb it with honey—on the fly."

I was never to harvest any honey. A month later I noticed that my bees were just buzzing around aimlessly. They wouldn't work the flowers.

"The CIO has finally gotten to the insect world," I said. "They're on strike."

A few days later the hive was silent. I went back to Guy Austin.

"All my bees are dead," I said.

"So are mine."

He said that the spray plane had done it. Zooming up and down the valley, a hired pilot spreading DDT against caterpillars had coated the countryside with death.

"There isn't a damn bee this side of Grafton," said Guy. "They won't touch the flowers. I guess they're starving to death."

The words sank in. The thought was somewhat stunning. Man murdering millions of bees in the name of progress?

"Maybe there's a spoonful of wild honey in the woods someplace," Guy added ruefully. "But you don't have a bishop's chance in hell of finding it—hah."

The bees gone, we returned to dull routine.

"We need something," I told Phyllis, as I helped her hang our diapers, "but I don't know what it is."

"Fewer kids maybe?" she said through the clothespins in her mouth.

At Readex a woman I had hired temporarily to help get out a shipment beckoned me to her car and opened the back door. Five puppies tumbled about in a big basket.

"The Chester Humane Society is selling them for a dollar apiece."

One black pup wagged his tail and said *wuf*. He licked my finger.

"Here's my buck."

On the jeep seat the little dog crawled over and poked a tiny, cold nose into my hand. All the way to Saxtons River, his eyes blinked at me worshipfully.

Pete and Mike jumped with delight. "Let's call him Duke!"

Small as a kitten, Duke was viewed with suspicion by the cats. Surely this was not a blood brother? Franklin D. Roosevelt stalked over, hissed, and gave him a cuff. Duke jumped. Then he wiggled in unmistakable glee and charged playfully. Within two days all the cats were his friends. Within two weeks he had won the heart of every person who drove into the gate. His joy at seeing the boys in the morning was so intense that he would squirm until his feet flew out from under him.

Throughout the summer Duke grew large and strong. He had none of the usual drawbacks of mongrels—stubby legs or misshapen head. Broad-chested, tapering at the legs, he was a beautiful collection of genes. A thoroughbred of his own.

Unlike Feather, he was not a fanatic physical culturist. He enjoyed lazing under our hammock, and that's where his games with Franklin D. always began.

Franklin D. would creep up, tail twitching. Assuring himself that Duke was asleep, he would leap on him and bite his ear. *Yipe!* Duke scrambled after him. The cat shot up a birch. Duke circled the tree, growling. Franklin D., seated on a limb, washed his face unconcernedly.

Finally Duke would lie down, ears drooping over his eyes. Half an hour later Franklin D. would descend slowly and Duke—speediest of dogs—would pounce on him. Oh, the yowls and growls, the flashing of claws and teeth! But neither antagonist drew blood. The drama would end with Franklin D. pinned beneath a powerful black paw and Duke calmly licking his huffed-up fur.

An hour later we might find them sprawled in the shade, Franklin D.'s head pillowed on Duke's muzzle.

People unfamiliar with the Duke-FDR routine were sometimes shocked. Once Albert Boni leaped up from our outside table, trying to shout through a mouthful of corn. He thought that murder was being committed. But it was only Duke stalking by, head high, with a screeching Franklin D. dangling—by the tail—from his jaws.

Duke brought us warmth, but still joy lagged. It was as if the Albino Mood remained. Here was warm, yolky June, yet the days were dragging like midwinter.

"We are two flat tires," said Phyllis.

A large, rugged young man appeared on the Knoll. He moved back and forth under our apple tree, looking upward, sort of tiptoeing in the orchard grass. He saw me, waved, and came over.

"You have a hummingbird in your Mackintosh," he said.

Then I saw binoculars hanging from his neck and realized that he was a bird watcher. We talked, I told him that an eagle had stopped by in the fall, resting on the topmost branch of our elm.

"I'm Chuck Blakney," he said, taking my hand in a powerful grip.

He was our Saxtons River minister. The conversation went this way and that, and I mentioned the disaster of my bees.

He said, "Bad if we keep tangling with nature like that. DDT is getting into the birds, too, affecting their reproduction."

He was a man of the cloth different from those I had met. He had been a champion wrestler at Williams College, and physical power was still evident in his movements. After he left, I told Phyllis we ought to venture downtown and see what other neighbors we had.

"Let's break a world record and go to church this Sunday."

"Okay anything," she said.

Our religious affiliation was Casual Congregational. It was impossible to live so close to nature and not be awed by the universe, but we preferred, as some poet once said, to "sail the seas with God alone." My idea of a reflective weekend was to hear wild music float up the mountain from Benson's Dance Barn two miles away on Saturday night, then listen to church chimes on Sunday morning. When the wind was right, our ears could catch hymns drifting from far-off steeples—the sweetest of sounds. A blanket in the sun invited us more than did an oakwood pew.

We went to church, with Pete and Mike, who fidgeted, and Christopher, who gurgled noisily. Chuck's sermon was simple and direct, and it got me thinking about things other than cement.

A few days later Chuck was back on the mountain with his young wife and a couple of babies. We talked about birds, athletics, and world religions.

"Hey, how about letting us use your knoll for a church service?" he asked.

The next week we worked—and how. Phyllis tore the house apart. She scrubbed walls and windows.

"If this place doesn't gleam, my name will be mud with the Colonial Dames," she said.

I scythed around the birches and on the Flat. When I started on the Knoll, Richard Bradley hitched Lexie and Prince to his mower and cut the whole area.

"I'll send Si over to help rake," he said.

We dumped the hay into our cellar hole. By Sunday the plantation looked as if an army of elves had groomed every nook.

"Another day of this," said Phyllis, collapsing on

her bunk, "and Chuck will preside over a funeral up here."

Sunday cracked over the mountain, yellow and fresh. The caravan began—sedans, jeeps, pickups. People I had seen but had never met poured out. Everyone was all smiles and handshakes. The men carried folding chairs to the Knoll. Duke romped with the kids.

The Bradleys came, bringing two sedate dining room chairs, and somebody planted an urn of roses beside the rickety lectern that Chuck set up in front.

It was an hour of the kind that just might keep the future church keyed to human needs—alive for the young. Chuck illustrated his talk with passing swallows and some frothy clouds. The odor of new hay drifted up. At the close, the June sun made a warm mix with voices singing "Jerusalem the golden, with milk and honey blest."

Afterward, card tables appeared under the trees, and the women unwrapped picnic lunches. People flowed in and out of the house, using the bathroom, getting water, and giving our pad the eye.

"Are we passing muster, Zeke?" said Phyllis.

It seemed so. After they were gone, leaving a tremendous emptiness in the still birches, we walked back to the Knoll. A rose petal lay where the urn had been. The hay was squashed in the cellar hole where kids had frolicked on it.

It had been a good show. Our lives had taken some kind of turn.

We didn't become steady churchgoers. But we started getting into things. Chuck went on a Canadian fishing trip, caught vast numbers of trout, and invited the whole town to a fish breakfast on his lawn. There somebody talked me into becoming Cub Master of the Saxtons River Pack.

"More boys?" said Phyllis, lifting a brow.

The involvement came none too soon. When I spoke at an organizational meeting, I found myself awkward and stumbling. The crowded room seemed unreal. It dawned on me that we had almost slipped into the position of "woodchucks"—curious folk who scrabbled around in the outback and gradually lost touch.

"The first Pack activity will be a track meet at my place this Saturday," I said.

A horde of little boys turned out. They wore pieces of uniform—an official shirt here, a neckerchief there.

"Number One Event—the around-the-apple-tree race."

They ran, stumbling and shouting. Pete, who was too young to be an official Cub, won.

"Number Two—the over-the-brook jump."

The afternoon roared by. We used a round stone for the putting shot, a bamboo fishing pole for the high jump cross-bar. At the end, we built a fire for hot dogs and marshmallows.

"I wish we had two million track meets every summer," said Pete, falling into bed.

Phyllis joined the involvement crusade also, taking day jobs as a substitute teacher at nearby Kurn Hattin School. The school was a sort of live-in refuge for young girls from broken families.

"You take Mike to Readex on the days I work," she said. "I'll handle Chris." Somehow this system operated. Then we got recruited for the PTA and, although the fall school term was two months away, I became Program Chairman.

By the end of June we were in town life up to our necks. The weekend before the Fourth of July I helped paint the firehouse, and Phyllis worked on a float for the parade.

"We're getting too lazy to hold back," I told Phyllis.

"Well, let's rein up, Zeke."

"We're trapped in the system now."

The Fourth dawned, hot as hell. The parade seemed to wilt marching down Main Street. The Grafton Band tramped over the melted tar spot where some youthful hot-shots had burned a car the night before. *Ta-ta-ta-taaaaaa* blared the trumpets. Here came floats pulled by tractors: a papier-maché barn with 4-H kids holding a live calf, a slabwood cabin with Boy Scouts splitting kindling. . . . Phyllis was Betsy Ross on the Mothers' Club float. In bonnet and ruffled dress she sat in a rocking chair and sewed the Stars and Stripes.

Then came kids carrying flags; kids pedaling bikes with red-white-and-blue bunting stuffed into the spokes; kids riding horses. Behind them a couple of sparse veteran units—from World Wars I and II—stepped along, toting rifles at rakish angles.

Whah. Rat-a-tat. Cars lining the street honked in approval. *Ka-wham!* A cannon cracker went off. Voices shrieked.

Finally the parade uncoiled and disintegrated. Saxtons River firemen dressed in bathing trunks began to haul big hoses onto Main Street. Opposite them, firemen from Westminster did likewise. The traditional Water Polo Fight was about to begin.

Moments later the two fire companies clashed. They aimed mighty streams of water at a soccer ball and tried to push it past the opponents' goal. Water flew in all directions. The ball jumped. The firemen ran back and forth, pointing the nozzles . . . missing . . . spraying spectators.

It was fun. I crowded close to the street to watch. Suddenly the Westminster team rushed up and a nozzle swung around. *Whap-wooooooooosh*—a stream of water belted me in the chest.

"Yeaaaaaaaaaa!"

"You won't need no bath tonight, bub!"

Dripping, I climbed into my jeep. Pete giggled at me. I drove to the Blakneys', where Mike and Chris were in a baby-sitting pool.

"That's what I call a baptism," said Chuck. "Fourth of July dew. Only first-class patriots rate it."

Moments later I had my revenge. The sky darkened. Lightning flashed, and a mighty cloud turned upside down on Saxtons River. People scrambled for shelter. I drove up behind the Mothers' Club float, which was hurrying into a barn, and took Phyllis off. She was soaked, her cheek stained with blue papier-maché.

"Head for the high ground, Zeke."

Back on the mountain, we changed to dry clothes. Then the sun came out, hot and humid. We drove downtown again and ate potato salad lunch in the church basement. Later there was square dancing in the street, a baseball game, a fishing pole raffle, and a sidewalk exhibition of paintings. By the time the band concert began on the school grounds, everyone was sweating. We sat on blankets and chewed popcorn. Babies squalled. Ice-cream cones dripped. Country ladies played bingo in a tent.

Independence Day, 1953, drifted toward the sunset.

We were too pooped to take in the evening dance at Kurn Hattin auditorium. Besides, Phyllis didn't want to park the kids with baby-sitters again. Instead, we sprawled on the Knoll and watched fireworks in the valley. Explosions blossomed and faded—lacy, flower-red. A second after they vanished, we would hear their delayed booms, like distant artillery.

"This has to be the hottest Fourth in history," said Phyllis, fluffing up her hair.

Not a breath of air came up the mountain. After the kids were in bed, lying naked on sticky sheets, we waded in Pete's Pool. In spite of the afternoon cloudburst, the water level was down to three inches.

"I've had enough involvement to last a bunch of days," said Phyllis.

"Me too," I agreed.

"People are nice down there, but it's nice up here, too."

"They key word is *balance*, Marthy. We've got to steer between two life-styles."

"Tomorrow let's find a place to swim—somewhere secluded," she said. "Just us."

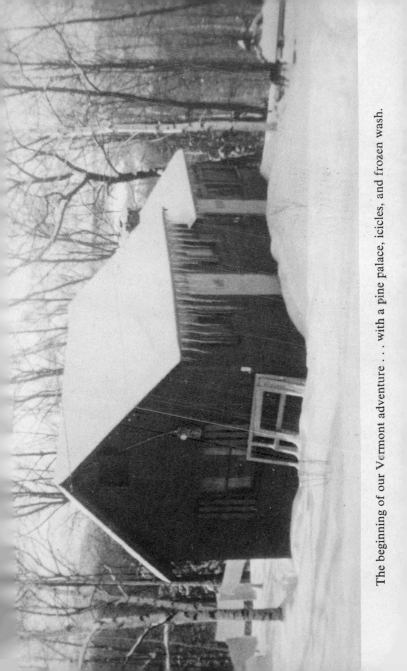

The beginning of our Vermont adventure . . . with a pine palace, icicles, and frozen wash.

George and Pete tracking through the birch grove . . . and Phyllis, "Queen of the Sticks."

Our homemade garage. A surplus army tent to keep the '35 Buick dry . . . Phyllis and Pete taking little Mike for a ride in the hand sled . . . Pete's pool, a hand-dug, log-lined swimming hole for those hot August days.

The mountain family grows . . . Phyllis and Baby Tim, Ol' Man George and Chris, Mike and Pete . . . Pete babysitting Mike . . . and a couple of years later Mike babysits Chris . . . Mike also gets to proudly test our barn-beam fireplace mantle.

When snow and ice surrender to spring it isn't long before the kids plunge into the water. Here's Phyllis and Tim (now 4) . . . and the rest of the gang doing their water sports . . . that last shot is Chris on top of Mike on top of Pete.

George toting a block . . . hauling a board . . . and building
another chimney.

Mike and Tim learn how to play with blocks—of cement . . .
as another addition to the shack takes shape.

We did it! Heated, painted, and mortgage-free! All it took was a lot of time, hard work, and love.

Plunging, Splashing—
and Trying to Stay Afloat

WE SEARCHED dusty roads within a radius of ten miles. At last, across the Connecticut River, we found a tiny lake buried in the woods. We changed to bathing suits and left Christopher on a blanket where we could watch him. Pete and I plunged in. Phyllis led Mike by the hand.

"Hey," said a voice.

A young man in a green sweat shirt came around the spruces. He had a catsup-colored, indignant face.

"You can't swim here," he said. "This is private land."

We apologized and left. The car bumped forlornly home. Pete tried to understand.

"He thought we'd hurt his land?" he asked. "Is that why he told us to go?"

I said, "Well—it's private property, and—" I stopped, perplexed over the way things are.

"Someday we'll have a pond, Dad," said Pete, "and we'll never tell anybody to go."

No hope, kid. But Pete's look, full of childish confidence, got me walking around restlessly. I examined the ruined dam across our brook. Poorly built, it had been undermined and toppled by spring freshets. Roots snaked over broken chunks of concrete and stone. The pond bed was full of mud.

My heart sank. From building Pete's Pool, I knew the endless hours of digging needed to construct even a small dam.

I said, "If I dig every weekend *ad infinitum*—and we don't get washed out before I get the dam rebuilt—we might finish in time to baptize our grandchildren."

"Why don't you talk to somebody downtown?" Phyllis suggested.

It was good to be back fiddling with a construction idea, anyhow, after all that togetherness with village revelers. I consulted some farmers. They were discouraging. A pond way up on the mountain? In vain did I point out our springs and usually running brook.

"You'll get a lot of water in April or thereabouts, but it will run out," they said. "Ponds work best in low country around here."

Then I glanced at the family exchequer and pushed the whole business aside anyhow. Was I crazy? The *Saturday Evening Post* revenues were nearly gone.

"We're heading back into the same old pit," I said. "And I can't seem to sell a story."

My dearth of sales, in fact, was becoming a real worry. I was employing an agent in New York—a dapper, cigar-smoking talker in a pinstripe suit whom I'll call Charlevoix. Five years previously, after my first *Colliers* sale, he had written me a restrained note on elegant stationery saying that he had had the pleasure of "representing Somerset Maugham, among others." Dazzled, I had joined his stable, and he had placed my stuff in various men's magazines at modest prices.

But since the sensational *Post* triumphs, he had sold nothing, despite my bombarding him with fiction.

"Until I hit a magazine, we shouldn't spend a dime on a pond," I said.

"You're the boss, Zeke."

I couldn't quite shelve the idea, though. *Our own pond—high in the hills!* Somebody suggested that I contact the U.S. Government agent in Brattleboro. I wrote, and shortly Fran Rohr, a big, confident engineer, arrived in a pickup. He assured me that a survey of our property was a free Federal service. If he found a suitable place for a pond, the Government would pay for the engineering; I, for the excavation.

He tramped around. He shook his head over the broken dam. "Bad construction. Wrong place, anyhow. The Government won't support private ponds that silt up like this."

I got ready to tell the family our disappointment.

"But," Fran went on, waving his arm at our swamp, "that place looks perfect. Five springs. Flat, marshy base. I'll bring up a drill to test the bottom."

The next weekend he and a helper took drillings.

"Perfect, indeed," he said.

With difficulty I restrained myself from turning a handspring.

We tried to be sensible. Grim and fiscal. *Wait until you get the dough,* said a voice in my head. But Phyllis sabotaged all restraint.

"Won't the pond raise the value of the property beyond any amount of money we borrow?" she asked.

I visited Z Persons once more. By all means dig the pond, he said. The bank would advance $1,000.

Easy as that. With a deceptive feeling of opulence, we watched a big apricot-tinted bulldozer plunge into the swamp. It peeled up rich black earth. As the hole grew, Phyllis and I walked around and decreed where the excess earth would be pushed. We created a dip here, a hummock there. It was like playing God, altering the planet.

Dry, hot days passed. Townsfolk came to stare at the awful cavity. Even Richard Bradley was dubious. He got Fran Rohr aside and chided him for squandering my money.

"He thinks it's going to be a dry hole," Frank told me with a smile.

The hole did look mighty empty when it was finished. The swamp around it lay under a four foot coating of new, raw soil.

"She'll be thirteen feet deep at the lowest point," said Fran.

Mud water rose, deep as a bathtub. It seeped in from two sides. Then my vacation came and we left for Connecticut. A week later we returned. Darkness had fallen, and I parked the jeep on the rim of the pond, its lights streaming into the brownish bowl. Pete ran down the sides, slipping on the mud.

Splash. "Water!" he shouted. "It's over my head!"

Thus Phyllis Pond (so christened at a later date) came to Hartley Hill. It was to change the lives of many people.

It was a quarter of an acre in size, and for a long time it looked like a gummy chocolate lagoon. I brought in two truckloads of washed concrete sand and spread them in one corner for a beach. Day after day we chopped at the lumpy banks with hoes and rakes.

Hoppy Dodge came up to give it the once-over. He said, "You can get free grass seed in barns. Ask Roland."

Aldrich and Bradley were glad to have us sweep up around the hay in their barns. We filled burlap bags with mixed seed. We sowed the dusty handfuls in the mud rills and it caught easily. In a few weeks the whole scarred area was shining with delicate grass the color of absinthe.

We swam—and found our brownish water cool and sweet.

It is a lesson to watch a pond from birth. At first it is only a wound, almost painful to look at. But gradually Mother Nature accepts it. The water clears. Vegetation creeps up to its edge. Wildlife saunter in. The first settlers are frogs arriving from nowhere and honking through the night. Then red salamanders appear. Then birds, usually starlings and flickers.

By the time cattails sprouted at the overflow end, we were finding deer tracks along the bank. Now and then a mysterious feather (hawk, wild duck?) drifted across the surface.

The summer waned swiftly. All of a sudden the glowworms' wink became feeble in the orchard grass and the twilights deepened to a golden brown. Sweaters came out again, and Phyllis and I asked each other: Where do the years go? Pete was starting school. Mike, chattering away, was racing through the house with toys and tools. Chris was rattling the bars of his crib and obviously plotting escape.

"Life is a struggle anywhere you are," said Phyllis with a shrug. "We picked here—and I'm not sorry."

Struggle was right. After our bold splurge, payments to the bank were crippling. I racked my brains and wrote and wrote. Still nothing sold. Phyllis looked into teaching. Saxtons River hoped to open a kindergarten soon, and she was first in line for the job. But so far, no luck.

" 'These are the times that try men's souls,' " I read from our dog-eared volume of Thomas Paine. " 'The summer soldier and the sunshine patriot will, in this crisis, shrink—' "

"Are any of those frogs big enough to eat?" said Phyllis.

Back to hard-rock economy. We stopped buying

anything but food and gasoline. I used old refrigerator sides to make gutters, the hood of a junked car as a stone skid. We scrounged for nickel-return bottles. Believing that progress on the property had to continue no matter what, we shifted our improvements to those that cost physical effort only—dry stone work and landscaping.

One day, while excavating a ditch, I hit a section of lead pipe. It was only a few inches down, running from a spring to where the old barn had stood on the Knoll. I hooked into it with the jeep, and—gingerly, so it wouldn't break—ripped up 100 feet of gray malleable material. I sold it to a scrap dealer in Walpole, New Hampshire, for $7.80.

I found nine used car batteries at the dump and sold them for a few dollars.

I started turning off the jeep motor on downgrades. Since I could coast nearly two miles on our road each day, plus another three on the Chester run, I saved a couple of gallons of gas a week.

And I wrote. Desperately, angrily—with a gnawing fear that my published stories had been flukes and no one out in the hostile world would ever care to read a thing I typed.

Charlevoix remained silent.

"Abe Martin was right," I said. "He said: 'It's not a sin to be poor—but it might as well be.' "

Phyllis draped a ragged towel over her head and picked up Chris. She waltzed around the room, singing, "Artificial flowers ... artificial flowers ... flowers for ladies of fashion to wear-r. ..."

We opened a can of lobster meat—last relic of our *Post* extravagances—and had a banquet.

"This will prime the pump," said Phyllis. "Get ready for good news."

Enduring

As WRITING FAILED, I did an impulsive thing. Deep in our back woods I hacked out a one-acre clearing. There was no road to it. I had to carry an ax through a swamp and along a ledge to reach the slanting, tree-choked mountainside. Nor was there an immediate purpose for it. Firewood, crying to be cut, grew closer to the house. (In this neck of the wild, self-seeding trees kept us battling for space to breathe, and a sensible man cleared his home area first.)

Nevertheless, one mulberry twilight in September, 1953, I started whacking ivory-colored chunks from a tall, gnarled hemlock. The tree tilted against a big maple, but would not fall. I chopped the maple. It came to rest against a rugged young oak. By this time lilac shadows had thickened. I had to leave the trees leaning—a dangerous thing.

"Don't go into the east woods," I warned Phyllis.

She lifted an eyebrow at Pete. "The Mad Axman is booby-trapping our property."

The next night I rushed home from Chester. I cleared the brush around the bowed oak and swung

109

my ax against its straining bark. CRACK. The green roof fell. Sitting in fragrant ferns, I saw a hole to the sky, threaded with dancing sparrows. Ah, breathing space.

"My clearing has begun," I announced at supper.

My wife and oldest son exchanged glances. Mike and Chris ate on, without interest, in their high chairs.

In the next five weeks I knocked down three trees each evening. It became an obsession. Often I chopped in cinder-soft darkness, my blade flashing like a mirror. During weekends I trimmed the fallen boles and hauled branches to the lower end.

Slowly the clearing widened. In late October, after snow arrived, I dug escape routes past the buried stumps. For I quickly learned that a tree, festooned with ice and wracked by wind, could fall any which way. As I fled from it, I couldn't risk tripping over concealed timber.

Friends looked in and shrugged. Only Richard Bradley seemed to understand. "Keep chopping," he said with a chuckle. "The reason will come out when it has a mind to."

By mid-November I had a battlefield. Crisscrossed logs jutted from sudsy drifts. Slugging with the ax and blowing ice-lace on my mackinaw collar, I felt muscles harden along my shoulders.

Sometimes I shouted for glory.

One cold Saturday, when the sky was slabbed with porcelain clouds, my ax skidded off a limb and hit my left leg. It was a glancing blow, missing the shinbone and not hurting too much. But blood trickled down my boot, red against the snow.

I was about to limp back to the house when the thought struck me: *What would an old Vermont pioneer have done in this situation?* I stood still, drinking in the harsh beauty of black-and-white hills. Then I pulled my wool sock over the wound and went back to work.

I *sensed* those long-vanished Vermonters around me. Watching. Judging. Like me, they had struggled to build homesteads on little capital. They too had shaped their property with an ax, because they hadn't had the means to do it any other way. How they would snort if I chickened out because of a mere shin scratch!

"I trust you're not going nuts," said Phyllis, bandaging my leg.

Thereafter, I was never alone in my project. The invisible settlers looked down. When a tree toppled, their ancient eyes seemed to assess its line of fall—its clean or gnawed-off cut. (Once a voice cracked, "Ax a mite dull?" I swear I heard it—or could it have been dead branches knocking in the gale? That night I sharpened the blade with a hand file.)

By December I knew what they looked like, those ghostly mentors. They were a trio—a red-faced shorty with thick arms, a bean pole with sinewy arms and no teeth, and a wide-shouldered Hercules who slouched against a tree, chewing something. All wore Colonial muslin shirts. All had lined, muscular faces. They hung around, indistinct in the birches. Contemptuous of my lack of plan, they began to put practical ideas in my head.

Now them trees are down, why not cut a road to pull 'em out?

As I stood considering the idea, Phyllis came up the snow trench waving an envelope.

"From Charlevoix," she cried.

The *Farm Journal* was interested in a story, but the editor wanted changes. I had written about a young PT boat commander in the Solomon Islands who had vanished, disgraced, in World War II. Several years later a Navy friend had come back to

111

find the commander a skeleton in his wrecked boat. But records showed that the commander's honor was intact, after all.

Could I switch the ending, asked the editor, so that the commander was found alive?

Could I? I abandoned the clearing and spent two intense nights over the typewriter. I rewrote the scenario so that the commander, dressed like Robinson Crusoe and living on coconuts, was found hale and hearty on a nearby island. It sounded plausible, and Phyllis said it was a triumph.

We sent it to New York. After an agonizing wait, Charlevoix's letter came back. I opened it with trembling hands.

Farm Journal says no. Sorry.

Back I went to the clearing, burying my disappointment with each bite of the ax. Shorty, Bean Pole, and Hercules were no help. *Why don't you render them logs fireplace-size?* Scorning their advice, I left the timber in crazy heaps.

"What," I asked Phyllis, "are we going to do about Christmas?"

She came up with ten dollars, squirreled away in a jar. We slaved over the Sears catalog, trying to squeeze toys and clothes for everybody out of the $100 credit ten dollars would bring. We settled for dungarees, slipper socks, and two toys for each boy, a camera for the family, and five-dollar gifts for Phyllis and me that we would pick by separate orders for the sake of secrecy.

Christmas sailed by, happy in spite of the pinch. The kids pranced in front of the fire. And the tree the Bradleys gave us filled the house with a rich scent of spruce.

February passed ... March. I welcomed knee-deep slush and thundering brooks, skunk cabbage and early robins.

My clearing emerged, tawny-wet from its polar mantle. Hoppy Dodge inspected it. "Why," he said, "you can't get any equipment to the damfool place."

"Exactly," I said, somehow pleased at the idea. That same day I felled four trees under the thoughtful gaze of my spirit friends.

One raw, slate-tinted afternoon I halted my jeep a mile below our house to glance at some tiny boot prints in the thin, velvet-new snow ahead.

They meandered like elf tracks. First, in a line, so ·················· ; then ···················· ; then :::::::::::::::::::::::::::: . I smiled. Translated, those cottony indentations told that Pete, trudging home from first grade an hour earlier, had (1) balanced on Ringling's high wire above cheering thousands; (2) become an airplane dipping its wings over the Arctic barrens; (3) turned into a rabbit *ka-whumfing* across a spongy Vermont meadow.

All winter Pete had traveled this route ahead of my arrival from Readex. His handiwork always offered something to look for: a snowball splattered against a birch; a few stones balanced on a stump, like a pagoda.

Phyllis and I had not worried about him, diminutive and alone though he was. The wilderness road was friendly. Log truckers waved to him. Hunters paused to chat. And he had been warned not to climb the banks of snow that protected the sides of the road from a steep, ice-choked gorge.

Shifting the jeep to low-low, I peered over the hood. The boot prints lengthened suddenly. Pete had started to run. Squirrel tracks appeared. Squirrel and boy had converged on a big oak. Then the boot prints circled the tree. The boy had lost the race.

So it went. A trailing stick had made fishtail squiggles. A rectangle in the snow betrayed where he had set down his lunch box to investigate a bare spot in the road.

And always the prints returned to : : : : : : : : : : : : :. Pete was some hopper.

Suddenly, at the Dows' farm, I jammed on the brakes and leaped out. The boot prints trailed over the bank and into the gorge.

Strictly forbidden.

I skidded down to the swift, gushing stream. The prints headed directly for the big culvert, made of massive stones, where the water tumbled under the road. I looked in—and my breath stopped.

Wedged between two rocks, its lid nodding half-open, floated Pete's red lunch box.

A chill knifed through me. Then I looked back and saw his boot prints go safely up the opposite side of the stream. Jumping from boulder to boulder, he had crossed the dangerous water but he lost his lunch box to the current.

Weak with relief, I followed the prints up to the road, then down to the other end of the culvert. They milled around the opening. Some broken branches showed where he had desperately tried to make a pole to reach the box. No luck.

Thereafter, the prints maintained a mournful sameness all the way uphill to our door: . . . .

"We'll have to punish him," I told Phyllis in the kitchen. She nodded. Neither of us wanted to think about what could have happened. The previous spring the stream had ripped out the whole road, dislodging granite lumps as huge as barrels. The water could be that fearsome.

"Please don't say anything until after supper," Phyllis said.

Pete was subdued right through his favorite dessert—deep-dish apple pie. He didn't mention his loss. Looking at his snub nose and downcast eyes, I experienced an annoying upsurge of arguments for the defense:

Aren't kids supposed to have a sense of adventure? What kind of spineless nincompoops would we raise if they didn't explore the wild?

After coffee, the sun glowed in coralline streaks on the western hills.

Parents can be absurdly overprotective. Are we?

I said, "It's still light enough to go back for that lunch box. Pete. Get the hatchet."

His eyes widened. Silently he slipped out to the garage, and my wife gave me a look that said, "You're chickening out, aren't you?"

"I'll do the disciplining at the scene," I retorted.

We drove through twilight stillness. Spring hovered above burgundy limbs and half-thawed fields. All of southern Vermont seemed to wait on tiptoe for one warm day, to break millions of wee buds and breathe incense into the air.

Pete muttered only three resentful words, "Daddies know everything," then lapsed into silence. Moments later we startled a deer, and Pete scrambled up on the seat to watch it vanish over a wall. I bit my lip. *The sweet curiosity of youth—a thing to be nurtured, not squashed.*

Then my mind shifted to a terror-stricken little wad of life tumbling helplessly in a white torrent....

Feeling half-miserable, half-righteous, I stopped at the Dows' culvert. My mouth formed the words. *Now see here, you deliberately disobeyed our hard-and-fast rule, and there'll be no movies for you till June.* But the sentence came out, "Cut a sapling about ten feet long, kid. We'll see what we can do."

It took half an hour to pry the lunch box loose. We scrunched down on a little ledge that slanted into the culvert and poked with the sapling. Crystal ice water gurgled and thundered. The culvert had been built

115

perhaps fifty years ago, and granite slabs that had worked loose from the overhead hung like monstrous shingles. It was a long, dark, moss-reeking tunnel—very time-haunted, very gloomy.

The lunch box bobbed out, swirling crazily. I managed to snatch it.

"Good, Dad. Good!"

We looked at each other—mountain guys who had conquered. In a split instant, our triumph shouldered aside the stupid relationship of disciplinarian and culprit. We climbed to the jeep, with water squishing from our boots.

Driving home, I hummed "Frosty, the Snowman," which was the song of songs that winter. Satin dusk had gathered along barbed-wire fences.

When our lights bounced through our wagon-wheel gate, Pete spoke hesitantly. "Mom will say good, too."

His eyes searched me in a kind of desperate appeal. They said, *Please let's not change the way things are now.*

Then, in man-to-man tones, he declared, "Boy, it's scary in a culvert. I'm not going down there any more."

"Me neither," I said.

We parked the jeep in our ghostly grove of white birches. Pete's hand slid into mine, soft as a sparrow. As we neared the house, I saw Phyllis setting mugs for hot chocolate on the mantel—her traditional offering for peace after a family upset.

When to be stern, when to be gentle—how do young parents know? This household will just have to play it by ear, bumbling along....

Outside the door, Pete began that infernal hopping again. He glanced up through naked branches, where diamond specks twinkled in a sky turning to tar paper.

"Are stars hard or soft?" he said.

April, 1954, arrived—a cold extension of March. Under clouds as gray as sharks, I worked on the clearing. My writing fell to a trickle. Given the circumstances, the tart criticism of my phantom friends of the woods was a relief.

Gonna waste this timber?

I cut it to fireplace length. Richard Bradley sent Si Finch to help with his chain saw.

You need a team and dray for hauling.

I got Jack Atwood, a logger, to bring horses and a rubber-tired wagon. Pete and I, and occasionally Phyllis and Mike, threw wood aboard. Pete rode with Jack as he drove the lurching, creaking cargoes across the swamp. We hauled out firewood that was to last for seven years.

Now what? We stared at the snag-toothed clearing.

"Let's level it for a hayfield," I said. "Bulldozer costs only eight bucks an hour."

Was I out of my mind? We were hoarding dimes for a long-wanted rug, a vital valve job for the jeep. But Phyllis just blinked—once—and said go ahead.

Within a week an orange-steel cat snarled through the woods, gouging a road. It uprooted stumps. It chewed down the high side of the clearing and pushed a huge hummock of fill to the low side. After two days the clearing lay bare, scented with raw topsoil. Beautiful!

Shorty, Bean Pole, and Hercules weren't carried away, however. *If you don't seed this muck-patch directly, it will go to gullies.* Okay, okay. . . .

Roland Aldrich agreed to harrow, sow, and fertilize the place for $200. I raised $50 by selling my cement-block maker—and pledged to pay the rest monthly.

"Just where are we heading?" asked Phyllis cautiously. I hardly knew. But even when Roland's big rogue tractor got stuck and a seed bag split open, I clung to our new-found obsession: This clearing had to be.

May slipped in, gauzed with green. Then . . . rain. Silver whips lashed pebble and leaf. The ground wrinkled. At the storm's end, gullies had grown to small canyons.

Plug them runoffs. Drenched and cursing, I piled stones in the muddy slots. By the time a drying wind appeared, the land was a washboard.

"It's a kind of sculpture, this clearing," said Phyllis. "*Earth Worried,* maybe?"

Our boots sucked water with every step. We abandoned the place for a week.

The day we returned—in brilliant sunshine—we got a delightful shock. The clearing had exploded in wild flowers—pink geraniums, snowy clintonias, yellow lady's slippers. New grass, emerald and soft, tinted the rills.

"Someday we'll fence it in," I said reverently. "Maybe we'll get a horse."

We didn't, of course. But as summer came on, we planted blueberries and dwarf fruits around the edge. When thick growth came up, I mowed the place by hand—stumbling in the small ravines, chiming my scythe against rocks.

We gathered no harvest to speak of. Yet I reaped a treasure from that damfool hole in the forest that couldn't be calculated in money or time. I worked out gallons of sweat while listening to the whisper of my blade. I inhaled the perfume of warm hay. I paused to chew grass and absorb the sky. (There was no next-door busybody to scoff, "That guy's the worst worker I've ever seen—rests every two minutes.") I sang, recited poetry, even cawed back at a crow who derided my music from a dead elm. I examined veins of lightning in a bloated August cloud—and puzzled over God.

Raking, muttering to myself, I stopped wars, climbed Everest, wrote deathless prose. Once when I learned that a dear friend had been killed in an accident, I trudged in misery over the bumpy turf, back and forth. Crickets sang. The sun moved on. Nature's sermon returned: *Everything is faithful to its cycle.*

I came home restored.

So the reason for it all came clear, as Richard Bradley had said it would. During those troubled months, I carved out that clearing because a guy needs a refuge in nature. His chemistry demands a private haunt to grapple with cold and heat, life wounds and soul weariness—a place to untether his most secret thoughts. In short, a place to be free.

A place to meet different sorts of friends, too—guys like Shorty, Bean Pole, and Hercules. Guys who materialize in the time-haunted woods, nod their tri-cornered hats, spit, and give good, blunt advice:

Got a middling-fair piece of dirt here, Morrill. It'll go to hell if you don't cut them hemlock seedlings.

Summer Snapshot

Once in a while, out of sheer perversity, I would not get up at 5:00 to write. I would lie in bed and listen as Phyllis brought the family to life. Her voice, soft as bells, floated from the crib outside our door where Christopher was coaxed into his clothes.

When the baby was small, she would wash him on a bathinette squeezed against my bookcases. "Oooooooo, my little babens!" she would cry, kissing his hands and letting her hair tumble over his naked body. The baby would gurgle in delight. I never grew tired of kibitzing on this mother-child interlude, but shortly it was only a memory. As soon as our kids could walk, she encouraged them to head for the bathroom on their own.

So, reclining in sinful laziness, I heard the shower go on, feet patter around, and Pete and Mike start arguing over something. The smell of cooking bacon drifted in. Then Phyllis leaned around the door, her cheeks freshly scrubbed and her mouth touched lightly with lipstick.

"Breakfast is served, Your Majesty."

"Has the coffee cream been warmed?" I inquired.

"Yes, Sire."

"Is the bacon limber—but not too limber?"

"Yes, Sire."

"Are the urchins out of the way?"

"The Princes are dining by themselves on the picnic table."

"What time is it?"

"Seven twenty-five. You're due at work in just thirty-five minutes."

Whenever I slept late like this, Phyllis made breakfast into an event. Sometimes she would bake muffins, studded with our own blueberries. Sometimes she would come up with a bit of country sausage, hidden in the freezer. We didn't talk about writing; we talked about practical things: the tiger lilies she was planting around the cabin, what to do about Christmas this year. . . .

It was a refreshing switch in the routine. And usually the day ended at supper with a blow-by-blow account of what happened on Hartley Hill during this special time, after I was in Chester and she was running her domestic show.

That night she said, "Boy, did this day blow apart, Zeke."

As soon as the jeep had chugged out the gate, she had drunk a third cup of coffee and smoked a cigarette. The phone rang. Could she bake a pie for the church sale?

"Okay. Chocolate chiffon?"

Bang. THUD. "Whaaaaaaaaaaaaa!"

"Mama! Chris pulled the plates down!" Pete cried.

Sweeping up the china with a broom in one hand and Chris balanced on her hip, she searched her memory for pie crust mix. Was there any in the house?

Mike ran in and buried his face in her skirt.

121

"What's the matter, honey?"

"We found a frog and he's *dead*."

She comforted him. Mike lifted tear-stained eyes. "When Pete put him in the hole, his heart was already up in heaven, wasn't it?"

Half an hour later, with Chris in clean diapers, sucking a bottle in his crib, she took the cabinet apart hunting for pie crust mix. No luck.

She changed the bed sheets, dumped the wash into the Bendix, and did the dishes. Pete and Mike appeared, and she made peanut butter sandwiches for them. She moved a pile of tools from the kitchen counter. She placed a gallon of yellow enamel, just bought at a penny sale, on the Bendix. She dragged the rugs out into the sun. She swept the floors. She found some story notes I had written on the back of several envelopes and started to stack them in the red bowl on the mantel.

Good Lord.

She upended the red bowl on a newspaper. Walnut shucks, bobby pins, thumbtacks, two ball-point pens that didn't work, two halves of a child's scissors, a rusty jackknife, a purple glass insulator—how did this junk collect? She sorted out half of it for saving and dumped the rest into the fireplace.

Pete came in. "I want to light the fire, Mom. Okay?"

She watched flames crackle around balled-up wastepaper, a Wheaties carton, and some egg boxes. The fireplace, she noted, was choked with ashes. It was high time somebody cleaned it out.

Later.

"Can we roast marshmallows in there?"

"I don't have any, Mike. It's sunny out. Go play with your trucks."

The screen door slammed behind him. Three cats ran for the kitchen.

She cleaned the bathroom and tossed a toothpaste box into the fire. She scrubbed the turquoise deposit under the sink faucet. She sank down into a sagging easy chair, but swiftly shifted position and removed a toy wooden milk bottle from beneath her.

This is a pretty room, she thought.

The furnishings—well, they were a hodgepodge, sort of Early P. T. Barnum to Late Charles A. Lindbergh. But the wide wooden arms on the sofa and chairs were handy to park glasses on. And the table lamps with their bulging clear-glass bases looked comfortably old-fashioned. The red curtains were a disgrace, faded and threadbare, but they were offset by the scintillant sword display along the mantel.

Maybe a couple of changes—

She experimented, pushing the desk beside the glass door leading to the bed-rooms. She moved it back. She shifted some Colonial iron candlesticks, a treasured present, from the knotty-pine console to the mantel.

Franklin D. jumped up onto the mantel. He took a swipe at a candlestick. It fell to the brick hearth, breaking in three pieces.

"Oh!"

She threw the cat out and walked around, shaking the iron pieces in her palm.

Nice going, you mangy home wrecker.

She went outside and took down clothes that had hung on the line since yesterday. She lifted the clothes basket—and the handle broke, dumping the clothes onto the grass.

Damned plastic. She replaced the clothes in the floppy basket and parked it temporarily on the grass. Then, warmed by the sun, she walked to the Flat, keeping an ear tuned for the baby in the house.

Suddenly Mike burst out the front door. "Mama, there's paint all over the kitchen!"

123

She ran back. Yellow paint was swelling over the green linoleum. In the middle of the floor, the can of paint lay on its side.

"Get Pete and bring some coffee cans from the garage."

They scooped paint from the floor with cans flattened on one side. Phyllis cursed herself for putting the gallon container on the vibrating Bendix. It had worked itself over the edge and had landed just right to pop the lid.

"Whah, whah—"

"Oh, Christopher."

Laying newspapers in front of her, Phyllis took sticky steps to the crib and changed the baby. She brought rags and kerosene from the garage. For the next endless hours, tatooed and blinded with yellow, she worked in the kitchen.

All at once the clock said 2:30. Thunder rumbled, the sun vanished, and a furious summer squall slammed into the mountain. The world rocked and boomed. Phyllis and the boys, gummy with paint, huddled on the sofa. She winced at the flashes, but tried to act unconcerned.

Once there was a simultaneous flash and roar. A tongue of fire shot out of the phone mouthpiece. She choked back a scream.

"It's clearing, Mom," said Pete.

Swiftly the storm moved on. It left a glistening world. Vapor floated from the woods, and water raced down the brook. The sun appeared, roasting hot. Phyllis went out and rehung the things from her soggy clothes basket.

What can I get for supper?

It was half a week to payday. Leftover time. She ground up a hunk of Sunday's pot roast and mixed in some beets—Red Flannel Hash. She took four eggs

124

from the cracked-egg box (half price at Mac's Grocery) to poach and spread on the top.

For dessert she sliced a two-day-old cake and made some hot lemon sauce to pour over it.

She was just dumping vegetable soup into a pot (two badly dented Campbell cans, 25 percent off at the First National in Bellows Falls) when the jeep pulled in.

"Some flap at the plant today," I said. "One of the arc lamps broke—"

She pushed me into a chair. Her face was flushed, and she gave a yelp of laughter.

"Now you listen. Just *listen* . . ."

How Zeke of Hartley Hill Tangled with a Villainous City Slicker

AUTUMN came early. Then everything went wrong. I remember the time stretch with particular poignancy because I had never seen such spectacular scenery—or experienced such cussed fortune.

The whole universe exploded in color. Day after day the sky was as blue as a welder's flame. At sundown crimson cloud wreckage littered the west. All over the mountainside trees glowed motionlessly, as if a billion elves had given each leaf a golden lick.

On top of that, the air had a dew-washed sweetness that almost made us tipsy.

In this jeweled climate, we got sick. Everyone came down with the upchucks, a rare occasion in our family. One never-to-be-forgotten night, each kid threw up at intervals of half an hour. In the middle of the night Phyllis fled to the bathroom, and a few minutes later I followed. We vomited simultaneously—she into the toilet and I into the bathtub—and it seemed that this duet would be on stage forever.

At last the humor of it got us. We lifted our eyes to each other, began laughing, heaved some more, gasped, and laid our cheeks against the cold porcelain.

" 'M-Moonlight in Vermont,' " choked Phyllis, naming the song then popular.

We were in sad shape for three days. Phyllis checked her kitchen for food poisoning and I examined the spring for a dead animal, but we found nothing. Bouillon and crackers gradually brought us around.

Then the floor furnace clogged with carbon and blew grime all over the living room. I took the whole rig apart and cleaned it with kerosene-soaked rags. Carbon black is one of the most insidious substances on earth. Fragile as a cobweb, it smudges to a dry prune-color that resists washing out. Although we worked with soap and bucket steadily, it was weeks before we felt really clean again.

At this time I also broke an ax handle, lost a crowbar, and—practicing football with Pete in the living room—fired a pass through our front-door window. Readex picked the same period to sink into another slump, and frighteningly—the film arriving from New York developed a fuzziness that made the microprint coming off the press nearly illegible.

Worst of all, my short story writing seemed dead. I still arose at 5:00 each morning to pound out a few paragraphs in my packing-crate office. Driving to Chester, I would try to continue the thought train, so I would have a start on the next day's effort. But the world took no notice.

One day a letter arrived from the *Saturday Evening Post*. It said that the magazine would no longer consider manuscripts submitted by Charlevoix. I was speechless.

"I wonder what happened?" whispered Phyllis.

I called the *Post*. An editor told me that Charlevoix had been pocketing his authors' checks. "He's a very slippery guy, and we're fed up with him."

I asked if the *Post* had told Charlevoix what it had done.

"We sent letters to all of Charlevoix's authors—and we told him we were sending them."

In a daze, I went to the post office. The postmaster handed me a letter from Charlevoix. Congratulations—I had just sold a story to *Argosy*. Check would follow.

"Something stinks," I told Phyllis. "He's trying to head me off."

"Why don't you call Mr. Boni?" she suggested.

Albert listened in his New York apartment. "You'd better get down here," he said. "Stay over with us."

I didn't even own a suit. In Bellows Falls, I bought a flashy tan tweed on credit. By raiding penny banks, cashing in nickel bottles, and taking part of next week's grocery money, I raised the price of a train ticket. Phyllis cleaned my ten-year-old camel's hair coat.

"Watch out fer them city slickers, Zeke," she said.

In New York, I called *Argosy*. When had they bought the story from me? "Oh, we paid for that six months ago," the editor said.

Six months. An agent is supposed to deduct his commission and rush the remainder along. In the shaky world of publishing, every Grub Street hack must have his bean-and-brew money without delay.

By the time I reached Charlevoix's fancy office on Fifth Avenue, I had lost my sense of humor. I kept thinking about Christmas in our snow-locked cabin and how we had struggled over the Sears catalog to stay within $100.

"I'd like to see Mr. Charlevoix, please."

I must have looked like Hairbreadth Harry gunning for the Villain. All three secretaries got up.

"Mr. Charlevoix is out," said one, a pretty girl with raven hair. "Can I help you?"

I explained who I was and said I wanted all my manuscripts. The secretaries moved around uneasily. What had happened? Surprised, I asked hadn't they heard about the *Saturday Evening Post* blast?

They looked at each other. "He's done it again," said the dark-haired girl.

She led me to a file cabinet. I was amazed that they didn't know what had happened. Hadn't Charlevoix's writers in the city shown up ahead of me?

She shook her head, smiling. "Authors are very trusting people."

It seemed that Charlevoix was always getting into financial tangles. He was an expert judge of writing, but he couldn't keep his hands off his clients' money. He backed plays. He lived well. Of course, he always intended to pay up. . . .

"Here's your file. Did you get paid for the *Philadelphia Inquirer* piece?"

No, I did not. Charlevoix had sold it three years before for $150. Fascinated, I ran through the file. He had sold my stories to various newspapers and small magazines. Fifty dollars here, one hundred dollars there. I felt heat rise in my neck when I came to the South Pacific PT boat story. *Farm Journal* had bought it for $1,000—before Christmas.

He had stolen $2,214 from me.

At a restaurant near Times Square, Albert said, "You need a lawyer."

Afford a lawyer—me? I decided to confront Charlevoix alone when he returned that afternoon.

Going up the elevator, I worked myself into a suitable rage—the Defender of Hearth and Home vs. the Starver of Babies. When I burst in, I was thinking: *Keep your head. Don't lose your cool until you've squeezed the dough out of him.*

"Mr. Charlevoix, you are a crook."

He barely blinked. But I think his cheek paled slightly. I put both fists on his desk.

"If I don't get your check right now," I said, "the next voice you hear will be the District Attorney's."

I had rehearsed the line for devastating effect. But he feigned surprise. Check? What did I mean?

There ensued a Grade B movie scene, with me storming around the office and threatening to punch him in the nose. The secretaries fluttered about saying, "Please sit down." "Please take off your hat." I lunged for the files. Charlevoix, alarmed, sought to protect them with his round, pinstriped body.

"Want to go to prison, Charlevoix?"

It was intense drama. But in the middle of it, despite my seriousness, I sensed interior laughter beginning. Part of me stepped back to watch the low comedy—and then and there I realized that I could never make it as a professional bill collector or a tough business executive. In fact, I was pretty far out of character as the straw boss of even a tiny plant like Readex.

Finally we got my file onto the desk, and I noticed—with satisfaction—that Charlevoix's hands were quivering. We added up the writing he had sold. He made no attempt to explain. He wrote a check, botched it, and tried again. He handed me the check for $2,214. A secretary brought me a package containing twenty-three short stories, and I got a list of others that were circulating.

"Send those to me the minute they come back," I ordered in my best Edward G. Robinson baritone.

It was ten minutes before three o'clock on Friday. I hurried to reach Manhattan Trust, Charlevoix's bank, before it closed.

"I want a certified check," I told the teller as I slid the green paper under the grill.

The check slid back. *Insufficient funds.*

"What I can't figure," I told Albert over the phone, "is how can a guy have a Fifth Avenue office and three secretaries—and not enough money to cover two grand?"

"Easily," he replied. "Now I'm getting you a lawyer."

He got none other than Philip Wittenberg, the eminent literary attorney. Wittenberg would take no fee, a gesture that was to become folklore in our family.

"This man is a menace to the profession," he said. "We mustn't let him get away with your money."

I endorsed the no-good check. Wittenberg took it, explaining that he had some influence at the bank and would get them to honor my check first, as soon as Charlevoix made a covering deposit.

I borrowed ten dollars to get back to Vermont.

Phyllis had a cold, the furnace was smoking, the rains had started—but it was good to creep into my mountain lair again. At least everything in it was real.

"Those skyscrapers look solid, Marthy," I told my wife, "but New York is all paper. Can't trust them slickers."

"That so, Zeke?" she said, sliding a mug of steaming chocolate across the table.

I looked up Byron Newton's poem about the city and read it to her with glee:

> Vulgar of manner, overfed,
> Overdressed and underbred;
> Heartless, Godless, hell's delight
> Rude by day and lewd by night.
> Purple-robed and pauper-clad,
> Raving, rotting, money-mad;
> A squirming herd in Mammon's mesh
> A wilderness of human flesh;

131

Crazed with avarice, lust and rum,
New York, thy name's Delirium.

She peered out at the dripping eaves. "Mmmmmm. Let's not get carried away, Zeke."

The next week the sun came out and the chill winds died. On Wednesday the money arrived. We stared at the pale bank check with its official scroll-work.

"Keep calm," I said. "Bite back tears."

Out of debt in one flash! We paid bills for cement, paint, lumber, shingles, pipe, and jeep repair. And Albert Boni got me another agent in New York, a respected professional who had once swung deals for Joseph Conrad.

Albert also gave me a lesson on the jungle world of business. "Did you collect interest on the money Charlevoix held back?" he asked.

No, I did not.

"How about damages for the wringer he put you through, transportation to New York, restaurant expenses . . . ?"

Nope.

The long-distance wire whined. "Humph," Albert said.

As for Charlevoix, his star blazed on. I had burned the damning evidence, his letter rejecting the *Farm Journal* story—and I wasn't interested in putting him in stocks anyhow. A few years later he uncovered a best-selling authoress and made money from her merrily. Then she happened to go to Greece and pick up a translation of her book that he had never told her about. . . .

The Friendly Time

DURING THE LONG SPAN when Charlevoix was sapping our strength (and trying my sanity), we kept our spirits up in various ways. For one, we reminisced a lot. By winter firelight, we hummed old songs and laughed at things we had done as far back as grammar school in Westbrook, Connecticut.

"Here we are, only in our thirties, and our memories stretch over twenty years," said Phyllis. "Boy, are we square."

We talked about skating at Cranberry Meadow when we were in sixth grade, skinny-dipping in Wright's Pond on summer nights. . . . We had been lucky kids, riding out the Depression in a town that still had unpaved roads and moonlit silences.

"We always got enough to eat," I said. "That impresses me more and more lately."

We delved into family history and even tried to trace a few lines. Phyllis's surname branch quickly jumped the Atlantic and vanished in southern Sweden. Mine, however, spread out mostly in Vermont, close enough to investigate. When we had nothing else to do—and had saved up a tankful of gas—we cruised around examining graveyards. We grew fond of those tilting, frost-cracked slabs of stone. So etched with joy and sorrow they were, so eloquent of earthly struggle and hope for salvation.

At last, on a lonely hillside in North Danville, Vermont, we found my great-great-great-grandfather Samuel, known as "Lieutenant Sam." The only things I ever learned about him was that he had marched in the Revolution and that his house had been "twice burnt."

Looking at the soft, roller-coaster hills that glowed with vetch and wild flowers, Phyllis said, "Why do you suppose the family left so beautiful a place?"

"The winters must have been brutal out here. Can you imagine how those old folk had to work?"

We decided that a seven-year war and the double burning of a farm were quite enough to fill a man's life six generations ago.

Sometimes our yak sessions would remind Phyllis of an old Swedish dish, and we would end up in the kitchen trying to re-create food she had eaten as a child. Sometimes I would regale her with stories about my ne'er-do-well Great-Uncle Charlie, who wandered around doing oil paintings wherever he could scrounge brushes and canvas. The paintings were lovely (my sister still has two). But Uncle Charlie never supported his children, and the aunts frowned on him. Whenever a schoolchild in the family showed any artistic talent, voices cried, "Look out—he's going like Uncle Charlie!"

On the wings of the New York check we set sail again—but cautiously. I got a motor overhaul on the jeep. Phyllis bought new curtains, straw gold this time so that they gave the whole room a sort of sherry glow.

134

One morning when the last tatters of snow were hanging along the road, Richard Bradley stopped me.

"Want to boil some sap?" he asked.

Si Finch hung old juice cans and buckets on the maples lining the road. We set a big steel tray, eight inches deep, up on loose bricks to use in boiling the syrup. We hauled in a pile of dead branches and some wood from under the barn.

"Takes one hell of a heap of timber to cook syrup," said Richard. "Shingles, old posts—like a that."

The nights were freezing, but each day the sun warmed the trees. Watery sap began to drip. Coming home from Readex, I would find Richard and Si feeding the fire under the tray. I would get out and help gather buckets. The fragrance of the bubbling sap, mixed with the scarlet chill of sundown, made me want to shout.

"Maple sugaring don't make much sense in time or effort," said Richard, "but it sure limbers up the appetite."

We walked around, smoking and telling jokes and dumping in sap. The stars came out. The fire crackled. Richard burst into his favorite song: " 'I won't live by a dam site with you-o-o.' "

"We're losing a few twigs in this mess," I said, dumping in a can.

"No charge for twigs and bark. They flavor the soup!"

Some time after the moon came up—a broken gold shell balancing on Little Baldy—we dipped spoons in the frothing syrup. We sprinkled granular snow on the tawny liquid and tasted it. Mmmmmmmmmm.

"Rake out the fire, boys," said Richard.

When the syrup was partly cooled, we funneled it into shiny gallon cans. I drove home with a can nestling warmly against my leg.

As soon as the ground was thawed, I hired three more hours of bulldozer time. The big cat crisscrossed the Knoll, filling in the cellar hole of the long-vanished barn where we had mined out old brick and flat stones.

When the job was done, Richard hired the machine for another hour—to level the ground on his side of our boundary line.

"He's going to knock down the boundary marker, but we'll fix that," he said.

"If he pushes it onto your side ten or twelve feet, no objection," I said. "He can leave it there."

He looked at me. "Yes, he can do that. A hawk can milk a cow, too—if it wears gloves."

The bulldozer roared in, obliterating the marker.

The following Sunday Richard appeared, dressed in a clean white shirt and necktie. Si was with him, carrying a shovel, a crowbar, and a cracked blue dinner plate.

"Ask Phyllis to give you an old plate," Richard said.

I followed them to our boundary line, holding a chipped platter my wife had willingly donated.

"Now," said Richard, "measure eighteen feet from that fence stone."

We measured. We sighted the line along the marker tree that stood on the Knoll. Every step of the way, Richard asked, "That right, George?" and "You agree?"

When we had the boundary decided on to the satisfaction of both of us, Si dug a deep hole. Richard broke his plate with a stone and sprinkled the shards in the bottom, and I did the same with my platter.

"That shows this is a property marker," said Richard, "like a that."

We set the crowbar in upright, leaving a foot and a

half above ground. We packed the earth tight around it.

"No lawyers, no surveyors—that's the way to beat the dollar devil," said Richard.

The ritual over, he invited me to his house for a beer—a cold one for me, the Yankee; a warm one for him, the Englishman.

The summer of 1955 came on. Crows cawed. Butterflies jittered over the grass like windblown gum wrappers. The sky turned a soft, smoky blue. For some reason the sunlight seemed brighter, warmer.

"This is a *friendly* time," said Phyllis.

It was that. When I hiked with Mike—a small, sturdy walker now—up Little Baldy, he said, "I can hardly wait to see my friend, the White Rock."

He referred to a snowy chunk of feldspar, big as two barrels, deposited by the glacier on the ledge top thousands of years ago. I had shown it to him the year before, when I had carried him most of the way up. It had filled him with wonder.

"The White Rock knows everything," he informed me with a wise nod.

When he arrived, he clambered up onto the glittery stone. He stretched out stubby arms and grinned with triumph. His happiness seemed to flow in all directions. It was as if the White Rock were indeed a living presence, a friend. Then I realized the vital bond between a child and his place—his turf. If our venture to the outback had done nothing else, it had given the boys a sense of territory. Each had a personal longitude and latitude to start from.

Mike got down and hunted among the small fragments frost-chipped from the White Rock. He found one shaped almost like an arrowhead and tucked it deep into his pocket.

"How big do rocks grow?" he asked, as we hiked down to the house. "The friendly ones?"

Our garden came up—not large, but packed with good eating. Si had plowed us a plot that yielded small ruby tomatoes, succulent peas, and other standard vegetables. We were not good farmers. (When we should have been hoeing, we were building bookcases for the house.) But at this particular interlude—while the whole universe smiled—even the weeds seemed reluctant to mar our joy; they let the produce sprout, luxuriant and tender.

One June midnight, while reading an evocative Thomas Wolfe description of food, I was seized with a longing for a salad. I lighted a Coleman lantern and walked to the garden. My glowing light flushed two deer, whose white tails disappeared out the gate like ermine muffs. I stooped and picked a pan of leaf lettuce. I yanked up some radishes, flecked with wet earth. I tore out a big handful of sharp-scented scallions.

In the kitchen, I washed the vegetables. I ripped the deer-nibbled lettuce to slender shreds, diced the radishes, and chopped up the scallions whole, from their pale bulbs to their slim, green tips.

After freshening a wooden bowl with cold water and shaking it dry, I dumped my garden treasure in. Then I mixed oil and vinegar in a jar, sprinkled it with salt and pepper, and shook it until it frothed. I laced it across my heaped-up greenery.

The next ten minutes were ecstasy. My tongue tingled. The crinkly ambrosia went down amid an orgiastic fandango of the taste buds. The elapsed time for that salad from earth to stomach was no more than fifteen minutes.

From that moment, all my future salads were to be pallid imitations.

We bought two outside lawn chairs, recliners made of aluminum and plastic. Their newness dazzled us.

"Henceforth," said Phyllis, lying back with eyes closed, her hands draped over the gleaming arms, "I am to be known as Queen of the Sticks."

We lay there for half an hour, listening to the hiss of wind in the birches. Suddenly a pickup stopped by the gate. Pete jumped out and ran for the house.

"Gotta change to my dungarees," he shouted. "Gotta help Karstens—his cows got the *bloat!*"

A few minutes later, he dashed back. The pickup went on up the mountain.

"What's the bloat?" asked Phyllis.

I looked it up. Cattle got the bloat when they ate certain vegetation—usually in excess. For some reason, the food mass fermented in the rumen or reticulum. Saliva stopped. The gas couldn't be belched or eructed. The cattle collapsed, becoming stiff-legged balloons that would die if they couldn't get relief.

"There'll be so much flatulence up at the Karstens' this afternoon, Pete will need earplugs," I said.

"Oh, boy—will his clothes be fragrant!"

We peered at each other speculatively. "This," I said, "looks like another gripping episode in the saga *Bill Karstens—Sodbuster.*"

The Karstens Farm—all five hundred acres of it—lay half a mile up the mountain. Its big part-stone mansion had been built by the Hartleys, wool millionaires of the early part of the century. In the old days, dances had been given there. Orchestras and guests from Saxtons River and Westminster had been hauled up the road by horse and carriage.

Suddenly the wool market had collapsed. The senior Hartley died, a rumored suicide, and his ashes were strewn around the fields. The property changed hands.

By the time we arrived, the mansion was a

deserted, mysterious place. Phyllis and I had reached it, ramming our old Buick up the water-gouged road, pushing aside overhanging branches. We explored it, wading through weeds around the massive stone ballroom. We found a door smashed open—and chaos inside. Rugs and furniture were strewn around. The fireplace was choked with ashes.

The next week, while in bed, we heard a truck fighting its way up the road. A sound like that was startling in such a remote place, and I snapped on the light.

Phyllis looked at her watch. "It's two thirty."

Who could be going to the mansion at this hour?

In the morning, we went back to the lonely structure. Its door was wide open. Double-tired tracks led up to the broad veranda.

"Somebody's *ransacking* this place," Phyllis said.

We found out that Connecticut people named Karstens owned the property but had not been around for several years. I wrote them a note explaining what we had seen, scrawled "Please forward" on the envelope, and dropped it at the Saxtons River post office.

Within two days they appeared, driving an expensive new sedan. The car churned its wheels helplessly on the ruined upper road. Mr. Karstens, a retired washing machine executive, backed onto our place.

"We've come to live in Vermont," he said.

Leaving the car, the Karstens—father, mother, and grown daughter—hiked to their huge, dilapidated house.

In the next months, things started happening there. Trucks carrying gravel, stone, and cement thundered up. Carpenters, plumbers, and masons appeared. A grader teetered over the mountain, widening the road and deepening the ditches. The Karstens scion—a rangy man in his forties named Bill—took charge of building barns and buying cattle. He lived out-of-state but came up on weekends. Since he owned a Chrysler agency in Connecticut, he could easily get his hands on all kinds of machinery. Soon the latest tractors and hay balers were parked in his sheds.

But then everything went wrong. The steep road was forever washing out. Bill bought an expensive bull, and it failed to breed. A culvert broke and left a truck carrying tons of lime wedged in a brook, its cab high in the air.

Month by month the unpredictable tyrannies of dry and wet weather made the Karstens's farming venture a nightmare. And now—here was the bloat.

"I hope," Phyllis said, settling deeper into the aluminum recliner, "Pete holds his lunch down."

At suppertime Pete trudged back, weary and redolent. Phyllis made him undress outside and dump his clothes into a bucket.

"What's the story?" I said.

"All of Mr. Karstens's Herefords busted through a fence. They got into the alfalfa and ate and ate. They were mooing and swollen up and lying around."

"What did you do?"

"I helped round up the ones still walking and eating. Then I helped stick the tube in their rear ends."

"What?" said Phyllis.

"You have to do that to get the gas out—and boy, does it come out."

Phyllis served the supper. "Well, let's talk about something else."

"Mr. Karstens—" Pete bent over his plate, laughing. We looked at him.

"Mr. Karstens . . . stood behind one . . . of the cows . . . and . . . BOOM!"

For several days the incident floated around

Saxtons River—to the amusement of all. "I'm glad everything came out all right," said a wag at O'Connor's Garage. "Karstens didn't lose no critters—and maybe he looks better in brown."

The Karstens Farm was never to make any money. Its plan to market beef through a Bellows Falls store came a cropper.

"It won't work," said Richard Bradley when the slaughtering began. "Beef critters don't fatten decent on the mountain—I don't know why. Western beef looks better on the counter. This here is *dairy* country."

He was right. Vermont housewives simply would not buy Hartley Hill beef. Eventually all the Karstens went back to Connecticut. Years later, Bill Karstens was to sell out to the Lincoln Land Development Company of Massachusetts, which had great ideas for opening up the whole mountain to home builders. For a while trucks and bulldozers rumbled through the woods, cutting roads. A new house arose at the mansion entrance. But this operation also flopped.

At this writing, another attempt is being made to make the farm work. Riding on a bankroll from somewhere, the familiar trucks are back. Horses and cattle wind up the road, peering out the tailgates of trailers. Perhaps the bold project will succeed. I wish it luck, but an insistent little voice in my mind repeats the words of economist Kenneth Galbraith, a Vermonter living in nearby Newfane:

"I have been repeatedly consulted by people who have had the dream of reviving agricultural production—beef production, potato production, livestock production—in Southern Vermont. I no longer adivse them not to do it because I found that when I did try to discourage them, they go ahead anyway.

"If people have the money to invest and lose in

Vermont agriculture, it's my feeling that they'd better lose it here than somewhere else."

August came, leopard-specked with goldenrod. The Friendly Summer, it seemed, went on and on. Pete and Mike built huts up the mountainside, with thatched evergreen roofs that hugged the ledge outcrops. They covered the floors with ferns. Occasionally I was invited to these wigwams to share peanut butter and crackers. We talked and whittled and drank lemonade out of a jar.

(It was here that Pete gave me a classic gleaning from his first biology lesson at Saxtons River school. "The food goes down your stomach and spreads all over. Some goes up in your lungs and head. Then the veins reach out and grab it.")

One day, walking down from a visit to Mike's hut, I saw an old woman, wearing a floppy hat and swinging a small black purse, coming up the Bradleys' west mowing. She looked exhausted—about to collapse—but each time she sank down, she got up again and came on.

Richard Bradley saw her about the same time I did, and we both met her on the Knoll.

"Why, hello," said Richard kindly. "Lost your way?"

The woman was Aunt Somebody, who lived at a farm on the Putney Road. She had wattled skin and a raspy voice—and she talked and talked.

"Why I was just out for a stroll you know isn't the goldenrod nice I'm tired I guess I'll just sit down here a minute thank you sakes the way times are you can't find a path in the woods fit to walk on my shoe hurts a little. . . ."

She half-collapsed in the tall grass, smoothing her cheap cotton skirt.

143

"Maybe you'd like to go over to the house to call your folks?" suggested Richard.

"Yes yes—that's an idea my grandson will come he has a red truck but the tailgate's broke he won't buy a new one he's got money too I wish they was horses like they used to be so a body could get around whew I'm hot now here's a dime for the phone call. . . ."

She turned the purse inside out. I noticed that it was a doll's purse and completely empty. She scraped and poked with her finger as she squinted in the toy coin compartment.

"There's a dime here I know there is my daughter put one in Christmastime. . . ."

With infinite patience Richard helped her into his pickup, saying that his wife would make her a cup of tea. They drove out the gate, her big hat bobbing in the rear window. The next day I learned she was a poverty case, living with relatives and running off now and then.

"When countryfolk wear out," said Phyllis, shaking her head, "where can they go?"

Well, they could go home, where, as Robert Frost said, "they have to take you in." But the twilight of life wasn't easy out here. I was glad when Richard told me that the relatives had come for the old lady all right, and they hadn't seemed perturbed.

"She has the run of their place," he said with approval. "She gets fed regular."

One topaz-and-jade morning in September, I was driving past the Barnes farm at the bottom of our road when a voice shouted, "Stop." A short man with white hair waved from the ditch.

I got out. He came up, wearing a clean turtleneck sweater and polished black shoes. He was carrying a pad, a pencil, a ruler, and a steel tape measure.

"Would you mind holding the end of this tape a moment?" he said in cultivated tones.

144

I held the tape end on various stakes he had driven along the road. He made measurements and wrote on his pad. He stomped around in the tall grass, his pants getting wet with dew. Then he sighted along a stake, stepped swiftly across the road, and made a mark on a tree.

I waited, mystified.

At last he came up, winding in the tape. "Thank you so much. It was imperative that I take these measurements before the sun rose any higher."

"What is this for?" I asked.

He explained that he was computing lines of magnetic force that offered a possible threat to the Barnes farm. Underground water, combined with the arrangement of surface stone, was an inducement to lightning. At certain times of the day, when the sun was at a particular angle, the peril was heightened by solar lines of energy. He was computing the components of the whole equation and would make a report to Mr. Barnes.

"He has a very bad situation here," he said. "See how the sun glints on that road sand, directly toward the barn? There's a magnum force line beneath the surface. He could lose his barn in a lightning storm."

I looked at the towering gray barn, which had stood for generations. "What can he do about it?"

"Several things. First, he can rearrange surface materials so that their refractive facets don't act as lenses attracting solar lines of power. Like this." He kicked some sand in the road. "Second, he can pile old rubber tires at the corner of the barn to act as insulators. . . ."

He talked on learnedly, smiling all the while. He commented politely on my jeep—how useful it must be on expeditions into Vermont's hinterland. Then he leaned close and half-whispered, "I have a good deal of material on magnetic-geophysical force lines that might interest you."

His blue eyes searched me. They had a twinkle, a sort of crack down the middle—and suddenly I realized that the man was absolutely daft.

I drove on, bemused. The next few days, every time I passed the Barnes farm the white-haired man was there, measuring fences and sheds, writing on his pad. He didn't look up, and I didn't stop.

Later I asked Harry Barnes about him. Harry, a hard-working farmer in his sixties, nodded. "Yep, his head is twisty. But he don't harm anything around here, so I just let him come and have his fun."

A week later the man was gone. He—and the old runaway lady—left me with a new insight into the compassion of our countryside. The odd, the retarded, the sick, the aged were accepted and treated with dignity out here. As long as they drifted about their occult affairs in peace, no one moved to stuff them into an institution.

Vermont, the general opinion went, *is the land of your youth and strength. It won't betray you when you are old.*

Thus the Friendly Summer waned. Fat, yellow-bellied fruit came out on our lone pear tree. Duke got ahold of Phyllis's go-to-church hat, a graceful gray felt affair I had brought her from France years ago. He ran around, shaking it. Phyllis shrieked, and all of us chased him. She got the hat back and patted it ruefully.

"That chapeau has seen its last church," I said.

She put it on. A hazel curl stuck through a rip. She balanced a piece of goldenrod behind her ear. "I'll wear it if I want. I'm Queen of the Sticks, aren't I?"

One afternoon as I chopped wood, my eye caught

sight of Phyllis hanging out clothes under the maples. The fresh sheets were billowing crazily in the wind, and Mike ran between them sniffing and stamping his bare feet. It was a pretty scene—Phyllis picking clothespins from her mouth with quick fingers . . . Mike jabbing the air, using a stick for a sword.

That night I dreamed the scene again. But suddenly the sheets turned into square stone slabs and began to walk. Phyllis and Mike ran from them, wide-eyed in terror. Mike started to climb a tree, which became a hole, sucking him down. Phyllis's face moved toward me, and her lips were rubbery clothespins that seemed to grow bigger and bigger, forming the words: "Mike is dead. . . . Mike is dead. . . .

I sat up, heart pounding. The cabin was dark. I bent over Phyllis and heard her even breathing. Then I investigated each boy. They were all asleep.

Throwing on a trench coat, I walked outside. It was a night to get drunk on fantasies. The trees had a patina of moonlight that made them practically transparent, and they were decked with pale stars. Glowworms winked from the grass. In the silence a silver bird shot by, a saber slash of wing.

Lovely dream.

Perhaps it was something I had eaten, an undigested bit of supper. I strolled around. The weird images faded. But I was now wide awake. Night thoughts—those reasonless musings that go with darkness and isolation—marched in, one by one.

You're in your thirties—and where are you going?

You've got three kids. Can you give them a start with the kind of money you'll ever get at Readex?

Are you losing weight?

Got to get new storm doors. Got to rebuild the spring. Got to sell a story . . . a story . . . a story. . . .

I picked up a stone, slippery with dew, and flung it

147

into the lower woods. *R-rip—crash.* I crawled back into bed and closed my eyes.

Is something the matter with me? We've never had a better stretch of time, a friendlier interlude.

I fell asleep just as wan light touched the curtain.

The Great Tool Drive

THE FRIENDLY SUMMER ended one chill afternoon when a cloudburst ripped out the culvert below the Bradleys'. I had to leave the jeep and carry three bags of groceries up the muddy road. It was like slogging over a battlefield. Lightning blazed. Thunder cannonaded.

I was about two hundred yards from the house when the sky simply turned over. Water *hammered*. The grocery bags disintegrated, and cans floated into the ditches. I arrived home choking for air and clinging to a jug of milk and some limp cracker cartons.

Then I discovered that a limb had gone through a window, and I had no tools to fix it. I tacked an old raincoat over the break.

"We're in great shape," I said. "My glass cutter has vanished and we don't own a putty knife."

The next day, cutting a piece of glass with the honed-down edge of a cold chisel and using a spoon handle for a putty knife, I made a vow:

I shall assemble an arsenal of tools and keep it in order.

"How do you propose to finance this dauntless operation?" asked Phyllis.

"First I'll sell our trailer."

Our chicken-coop-on-Ford-wheels, which had first moved us to Vermont, had done its duty. We were no longer making hauls from Connecticut. To Phyllis's astonishment, I found a guy who gave me three ten-dollar bills for it.

"Now watch," I said.

I started visiting barns. I would ask the owner if he had any old tools he wanted to sell. Often he would bring out an oil-stained boxful, and I would buy it for two or three dollars.

At home I would dig through the mess, throwing hopeless junk into a scrap pile. What treasures came to light! A nicely balanced ball-peen-hammer head, a vise with only the twist bar missing . . . I shaped a new handle for the hammer from a broken ax handle. I fitted the vise with a spike for a twist bar.

As the barn findings accumulated, I discovered that I could use odd parts from one box to make, or improve, tools from another. A short piece of pipe clamped over the handle of a monkey wrench gave me a high-leverage tool. Some chisel handles, bored at the end, became excellent hilts for steel files.

Piece by piece my arsenal went up on the wall over my long plank workbench. Gradually I found that I could reach for—and find—a tool that fitted a job without having to improvise. I stopped sharpening half-inch bolts for chisels and using Phyllis's scissors to gnaw through No. 14 electric wire.

One day when we were leveling off several loads of fill on a slope where we wanted a lawn, my father-in-law, visiting from Connecticut, said, "Why don't you make a grader?"

Sure. I'll set up a machine shop and go to it.

I left for a couple of hours. When I got back, my

sons were pulling a contraption made of plywood and lathes along the slope. It was a simple grader. Each time they passed over a pile, the wooden blade hauled some fill with it. They were "playing horse" and laughing.

"That's better than shoveling," said my father-in-law.

He had nailed it together from bits of scrap. I picked it up. It was light but strong. A simple, primitive thing, it was going to save us hours of dull labor.

"Pretty classy."

The grader started my mind down a new track. Weren't there other timesaving devices I could put together—homemade tools? I built a tamper out of a log nailed with bedslat handles. I fastened heavy screen onto a frame so I could sift my own concrete sand from cheap bank gravel.

One day I scrunched under the west side of our house, beside our massive chimney, and tried to figure out the easiest way to excavate the place for a cellar. There was headroom of about four feet in front, diminishing to twelve inches as I crawled back. There was nothing to do but start working with shovel and crowbar, heaving the earth as far as I could.

But that meant that I would have to move the earth again as it piled up—and move it still more times the farther I got under the house. Wasn't there a way to shovel it once and haul it off?

Well, the classic answer was a wheelbarrow. But a wheelbarrow doesn't hold much, and the thought of pushing a loaded wheelbarrow over inclines and dips was discouraging.

Then a light bulb went off in my head.

I got a big engine hood from a junked Cadillac. I bored holes in its nose, bolted some tire chains to it, and hitched my one-inch Manila line to the chains.

Dragged, upside down, under the house, the hood

became a large bucket, open at the back end. I shoveled it full of dirt—about three times the size of a wheelbarrow load.

Next I fastened a pulley block to a big beech tree hanging over the bank about seventy feet from the excavation. I put it twelve feet off the ground. I rove my Manila line through the block and angled it out to flat land beside the garage. I hitched it to the rear frame of the car.

"Watch," I told my dubious family.

I pressed the gas. The line tightened. The brimming hood skidded out from under the house and traveled bumpily to the beech tree. It climbed up the pulley, dumping its load automatically over the bank.

"The Barefoot Archimedes strikes again," said Phyllis.

I backed the car up, and we dragged the hood under the house again. The rig was to save us a century of sweaty work.

Richard Bradley looked with approval at my growing array of tools. He had started to build himself a new house from timber he and Si were hauling off Big Baldy and trucking to Tenney's Lumber Mill.

"Gonna sell my cows and retire next summer," he said. "People tell me to move to town, but I'm coming higher up the mountain."

A machinist before he became a farmer, Richard was interested in any kind of contraption that would ease man's passage through life.

"Years ago a feller brought the damnedest conglomeration of wheels and belts up here," he said. "The Universal Hay Drier—built it in his barn, I guess."

Watched by an assemblage of bankers and farmers, the inventor hitched his machine to a horse. He lighted a dozen kerosene burners fixed underneath a broad, flexible metal belt. The idea was that when the machine was pulled forward, wire fingers would pick up mown hay and deposit it on the moving belt. As the hay crossed the burners, it would dry and fall out behind.

"If the thing worked," Richard said, "a farmer could make a cutting, dry it, and barn it, without needing the sun at all."

"How did it work?"

He chuckled. "Wal . . . this inventor feller kept running behind, picking up hay and shouting to the bankers, 'Dry as a bone!' I picked up some, and it was hot on the surface and wet underneath."

The Universal Hay Drier lumbered across Hartley Hill. At the end of the row, the horse turned. The driver got his reins tangled momentarily, and the whole rig stopped.

"The hay on the belt began to smoke," said Richard. "The inventor hollered, 'Giddup! Giddup!' Just as the driver got going again, the hay caught fire."

He bent, laughing soundlessly.

"Gee God! The fire shot up. The horse saw it and took off. Bumpilty-bang, that old hay drier hot-stepped around, dropping fire everyplace. The driver couldn't do nothing but jump off. We ran all over the place stamping out fires."

At last the hay drier hit a gully and broke apart. The horse ran away, dragging its traces.

"We warmed our hands over what was left of that contraption. Didn't see that inventor feller again."

Richard advised me to make a repair bin. "Just a big box to throw an ax in when the handle goes or a saw when it calls for sharpening. Come bad weather, you got all your inside work in one place."

I set aside a section under my bench. It filled up and stayed that way, despite periodic efforts to empty it. Tools, I was learning, would steadily break, wear out, grow dull, and bend out of shape. Into my repair bin went stray nuts, bolts, radiator straps, screws, ax wedges, wire, glue—anything that could conceivably be used to fix a tool. Richard proved right. The bin brought order to my tool operation.

Anytime I heard of an auction within five miles, I went. I searched for tools, decided the limit of my bids (very low), and stuck to them. Often, ancient tools came up on the block. If they were quaint items beloved by antique hunters, such as ox yokes or hand-hewn bucksaws, I left them alone. But if they were prosaic things such as crowbars or tin snips, I was interested. I bought adz and broadax heads. I bought huge, handwrought ice tongs of great strength which had once been used on frozen ponds.

I even bought an old box of cobbler's tools, too battered to be of interest to antique collectors but containing several sharp instruments that proved useful in repairing belts and tarpaulins.

One afternoon Richard Bradley, his grown son Ray from Massachusetts, and Si came over, carrying some long lengths of heavy 2-inch pipe.

"We want to use your twin oak for bending," Richard said.

A tall oak, with two thick trunks rising in a V, stood behind our house. I had never looked on it as a tool before.

"Oh, yes," said Richard. "A forked tree is a great asset to your property—if it's strong enough."

He inserted the pipe into the gap. "Okay, boys, push—easy." We leaned on the long end of the pipe. It bent.

"Hold it! Slack up."

Richard kept moving the pipe along bend marks penciled on its surface. Gingerly, we pushed, and the pipe began to arch gracefully. We made two lengths, identical in contour. Richard took them home and fitted them as perfect railings for his new front steps.

"My eyes are open," I told Phyllis. "Work-saving implements actually *grow* on Hartley Hill."

"I'll tell you one that isn't growing here," said Phyllis, pushing a carton of boys' worn-out sneakers through the back door. "A *girl*."

I built a sawhorse from scrap lumber. I laboriously leveled off a big stump for a chopping block. When I chanced on an ironwood tree with an unusually straight, smooth bole, I cut it up into lengths to use as rollers. Thereafter, heavy boxes or a refrigerator could be moved with ease on our floors.

With the boys, I built an outside worktable on an elm stump. Planked with 2-inch oak and ringed by pieces of trunk for seats, the table gave us a place to do repair jobs under leaf-filtered sunlight.

Without realizing it, we gradually learned to use one of the best tools of all—gravity. For a long time, we puzzled over how to build a dock for the pond. Creosoted timbers? Oil drums?

"Stone is best," said Pete.

True. But how could we lug boulders weighing hundreds of pounds?

We tramped over the property. Along the road leading to the mansion, large stones fringed our border. They rested high above the pond.

"Can't we drag them?" asked Phyllis.

One day, at the Cold River Stone Crushery in New Hampshire, I saw some rusty screens, five feet square. Discards from the traprock sorting mechanism, they were thick and strong, made of the toughest steel.

"How much do you want for one of those old stone screens?" I asked.

"Oh . . . three bucks."

I bought five screens at two dollars apiece. At home, Pete and I chained one behind the car and drove up to the big stones. We crowbarred a massive chunk onto the screen and hauled it to the upper bank of the pond.

Using this simple stone-boat, we assembled enough huge gray lumps to build a dock. Then the whole family simply sat and pushed against the stones with our feet. The stones edged into position, going downhill all the way.

Gravity had done 75 percent of the work.

Fire became useful, too. I was forever finding parts of wagons or sleighs covered with good steelware imbedded in pieces of oak. I would have to work for hours to separate the useful metal from the useless wood. But, when the pieces were tossed in the fireplace while a good blaze was going, the bolts and plates would be burned clean.

After a while, raking out the ashes became a kind of treasure hunt, since every few weeks I would forget what I had consigned to the flames.

I also tried to find a way to use the wind for a tool. Some days the trees thrashed with invisible force, and often the gusts were so strong that they tore down branches. The Bradleys, bothered by moles, discovered that small, homemade windmills stuck in their lawn kept the pests away. The endless vibration evidently annoyed denizens of subterranea. But, since we had no moles, I never found a purpose for harnessing Hartley Hill's gorgeous breezes.

"Building a windmill will have to wait until I get the dough to finance a big one for power," I said.

"Which will have to wait," added Phyllis hastily.

Clamps, wrenches, hatchets—tools flowed into our garage. Some were mere lumps of rust when they arrived. We went to work on them with sandpaper and Liquid Wrench. Some of the old ones—relics of another age—proved astonishingly useful. Old-fashioned wooden planes turned out to be fine workers, once we became accustomed to their bulk. Blacksmith tongs could be employed in a hundred different ways, from fishing metal out of the fire to towing a skunk carcass to a dug hole. And a handwrought peavey proved absolutely the best means of rolling logs.

As the wall over my bench filled up, I gained in confidence. Hacker I might be—sloppy carpenter, Rube Goldberg machinist—but, armed with the right tool, I was not to be dismissed out of hand. I could assault almost *any* job. And victory was possible.

Autumn deepened, chartreuse and russet. A wedge of geese flew south. In the morning, I would find a dusting of frost on the fringed gentians.

One twilight, driving home from Chester, I saw a Vermont farmer leaning on the fender of his truck. I stopped.

"Radiator hose busted," he said. "I got a new piece, but of course my tools are in the pickup at home."

The afterglow shone on his rugged face. He had wide, powerful hands, grease-nicked from working on farm machinery.

"I got tools," I said.

I pulled down the jeep's tailgate. For a wonder, the night before I had rearranged the hodgepodge of equipment a Vermont countryman customarily carries.

My toolbox was open, neatly packed with pliers, screwdrivers, hose clamps, hammers, files, wire, an adapter, a metal punch—everything. My hatchet lay alongside. On a cushion of burlap rested a skill saw, power drill, sander, battery charger, chain saw, and hand pump. Along the tailgate stretched a towing chain, two jumper cables, and a hydraulic jack. And, over the spare tire, hung forty feet of Manila rope.

The whole spread had a soft, oily gleam, like a display in a hardware store window.

"That," said the farmer, bending over, "is a *comforting* sight."

157

The tool caper was a victory, no doubt about it. But for some reason it didn't fill a peculiar void that—to my disgust—was growing in me. I had noticed it ever since my dream about Phyllis and Mike. There had been other dreams, equally senseless, that involved myself. I was running across empty deserts, or I was in the cabin and it was pulsating and twisting—things like that. They added up to a burgeoning distraction from the Plan.

Why this abridgment of joy? How come I wasn't getting the same kick out of small, hard-won accomplishments that I had gotten in the days when we had been installing electricity or building the ell?

I said nothing to Phyllis. But I did a lot of stern talking to myself. Good God, man, you're doing what you wanted, aren't you? You've committed a whole family to this outback life-style, and they're thriving. What's the bitch?

I shifted my reading to humor stories—Mark Twain and light fiction in the magazines. I stopped writing World War II pieces and tried some love-adventure. A couple sold, and the checks were sizable. But I looked at them and felt no particular emotion, no urge to turn a handspring.

Holy cats, are you developing into a sourpuss?

Driving to Chester, I gazed silently at the beautiful molten hills smeared with red and gold. My eyes were drawn, however, to the tormented bodies of elms beside the road. Stripped of bark by the Dutch elm disease, sticking up like pegs, they symbolized everything dismal. I got into the habit of counting them, trip after trip.

What you need, said a voice in my head, *is a new project—something tough to throw your whole energy into.*

"You Are a King by Your Own Fireside, as Much as Any Monarch in His Throne."

—CERVANTES

"It's GETTING COLDER," I said. "Working conditions will be lousy. It's time to start a chimney for the ell."

"That figures," said Phyllis.

"We mustn't do it the bright way. In summer."

"Nossir. Don't give any false impressions—like we have brains."

The stones were piled up, ready to go. I had junk lumber for scaffolding. Our first fireplace had been so successful, heating the cabin to livable temperatures when the outside thermometer read 20-below, that we had become fireplace freaks. *Everyone* in the sticks, we believed, should have one. Now we wanted a second, placed in the ell next to the picture window. We needed a fireplace for protection in case our furnace konked out during a three-day blizzard. We needed it to restore elan after two weeks of no sunlight.

A crackling fire is company in the room. For children, glowing coals are the incubators of dreams.

The practical uses of a fireplace are endless—incinerator for waste, forge in which to bend metal, emergency lamp, emergency stove. In a man's most threadbare moment, he can chop up some dead branches and bring his hovel to life with frisking colors of delphinium, sunflower, and bloodstone—all trapped safely behind a fire screen. And the burning wood spices his room with sweet aromas of the bosk.

Our first fireplace and chimney had cost us exactly $177. This included cement, sand, tile (for two flues), labor by Al Williams at $1.25 an hour—and a Heatilator unit. Cheap enough, considering that my sweat was free.

(The Heatilator has long since taken the guesswork out of fireplace building. It is a shell of heavy steel welded in exactly the right contours to give the firebox a smokeless operation. You simply build your stonework or brickwork around it. It's really a "stove" that will throw many times more heat than a masonry-back fireplace. Two flues at the bottom suck in cold air. The air circulates upward in a steel chamber behind the firebox. It emerges from two flues at the top, hot as the Devil's breath.)

I started chipping cement from used bricks and stacking them in separate piles—ugly ones for work that wouldn't show, handsome ones for display along the front. This fireplace, like the other, would be built of old brick; the chimney, of stone.

Pete and I dug the foundation. Seven now, my firstborn son was stocky and strong, a pint-size workhorse who got involved in every construction job that came along. In the building of the earlier chimney he, barely three years old, had astounded us by mixing cement with me for hours. Now he was robust enough to carry bricks and pound scaffolding together.

We dragged in steel reinforcing from all over—L-bars cut out of bedsprings, pieces of pipe, car parts, and rusty cable.

We got insulation from a couple of junked refrigerators. It was the very best—batts of 1½-inch fiber glass, dry as husks despite years of abandonment. As we took apart the beautifully built old boxes, we saved the stainless steel metal screws in a coffee can to use in fastening the flue extensions.

The foundation hole deepened rapidly. We went down three feet, then added another foot for "Ignorance Factor." Ignorance Factor? That was a "margin" that our five years of struggle on the mountain had taught us to use on all projects. It was the extra bit we put into any construction to allow for our limited experience. An extra nail, we reasoned, might compensate for a poorly positioned two-by-four. An extra winding of tape might protect an amateurish electrical connection. The idea had served us well.

When the four-foot cavity was squared off at the corner, we started filling it. A mason had told us long before that an 8 to 1 mixture of concrete was okay below the ground; that is, 8 shovelfuls of sand to every 1 of Portland cement. We subtracted an Ignorance Factor of 2, making the ratio 6 to 1. It was a long job. We mixed concrete by hoe in our old sleigh body, dumped the gooey mess in, and then dropped big rocks.

We took care to get rid of only the odd-sided, lumpy rocks that would be difficult to work with above ground. Before dropping each rock, we dipped it into a water-filled oil drum, since stone binds better when wet.

By this time hunters were prowling over the mountain. Grouse sailed under trees that glittered in gold and vermilion. Now and then a shotgun blasted. The taste of the air was cold, leafy—and we had to keep moving to stay warm.

Phyllis came out, tucked in a Navy jacket, to help move bricks.

"Let's not put up the scaffold till it snows," she said, "so we can slip on it."

I nodded. "And the temperature falls enough to freeze the concrete."

"And we catch cold."

"And the money for Christmas has wasted away."

She addressed the sky. "Operation here has flipped out, Lord. Drop the net."

But we kept working. After racing home from Readex, I toiled in the failing light before supper. Once the chimney had risen above ground, we mixed lime with the cement to make it adhere better. (Masonry cement, requiring no additive, could be bought, but I was stuck with the regular, since I had bought fifty bags off a freight car in Bellows Falls in a special deal.)

Mix mortar. Heave stones. Smooth the joints with an old tablespoon. Days went by in a blur. We were back to the early rhythms, racing to finish before a blizzard hit the hill.

"We're gyrating fools," said Phyllis. "I feel like a revolving door."

She had opened Saxtons River's first kindergarten. Each weekday I dropped her off at the village school on my way to Chester. We had a baby-sitter for Mike and Chris, a jolly Vermont girl named Jeanette. The house was full of comings and goings, lunches and snacks, clothes-washings and kid-tumblings.

"If we get this chimney to the top, we'll celebrate," I told Phyllis. "A cup of coffee and a three-minute self-congratulation break."

"Dissipation like that brought Rome to her knees, Zeke."

Wisps of snow started. I hired Al Williams again to work on weekends. The chimney reached our noses, and we cut into the house wall. We sawed into the floor for a hearth. A hearth should stand alone. If its weight rests on the floor joists, you are asking for it to crack or sag. We trimmed the 2-by-6-inch joists down two inches in the hearth area and nailed a rough "tray" of old corrugated roofing there. Then we positioned steel L-bars, cut from bedsprings, in the tray, with their ends extending from the front of the hearth to the back side of the chimney. We poured concrete over the L-bars, filling the tray, and we built up the back side of the chimney a couple of stones so that its weight, resting on the L-bars, supported the hearth.

Now, the higher the chimney went, the more strongly it would hold up the reinforced concrete of the hearth.

By this time we were fastening blankets over the gap in the wall at night to keep out November gusts. Pete and I wrestled the Heatilator into place and started bricking it up. We threw up a scaffold of barn lumber, and I spiked in some extra two-by-sixes for Ignorance Factor.

The days shortened. Evenings, Pete and I used a battered bridge lamp for light. We wet down the Heatilator and plastered it with insulation batts from the old refrigerators. (Without insulation to keep mortar from touching a Heatilator, the Heatilator's metal will expand in a hot fire and crack the fireplace bricks loose.)

We laid up the bricks. At mantel height, we positioned an 8-by-8-inch beam salvaged from Readex's cellar. I chiseled two 4-by-4-inch holes in it and ran 14-inch bolts through them into the chimney cement to secure it tightly. Then I concealed the bolts by plugging the holes with stubby 4-by-4-inch pieces.

There stood an antique-brick fireplace, topped by a roughhewn mantel.

Phyllis was ecstatic. It was beautiful—beautiful. But

I looked out at the flue-tile sticking up from stumpy, jagged stone.

"It's ten miles to the roof," I said. "Pray for tropic weather."

Our job was only half done—the easy half. Now the chimney had to be built up from the fireplace along the outside of the house. It was a long, long way to go. And the flue had to top out two feet above the ridgepole; otherwise, the fireplace might smoke.

The next two weeks were hectic. Every spare moment, sleet or shine, we zeroed in on the chimney. We built a second—and finally a third—platform on our scaffold. Since the higher we went, the higher I pushed our Ignorance Factor, we pounded a lot of timber into that thing. Construction slowed radically as we got off the ground. Snow had to be swept from the platforms. Everything had to be lifted—stones, concrete, tools. We built a boom with a pulley on it, but found it quicker to lift our stones from platform to platform by hand. Al mixed concrete below and kept me supplied by bucket. The wind whistled. Our hands grew wrinkled. But somehow the chimney inched upward. At night we protected the new concrete from freezing with burlap bags.

As with the first chimney, we didn't bother with guide strings. In our rustic homestead, I saw no need to be picky-precise. I just heeded the advice that Hoppy Dodge had given us four years before:

"With each layer of stone, stand off and look at the thing, and make corrections on the next layer. If you just keep piling stone on stone without looking, you'll commence to get into trouble. You may be only an inch off on the bottom; but by the time you reach the top, you'll be over in Bellows Falls."

Up . . . up. A bitter chill moved into the valley and hung on. Ice skimmed over the water barrel. The chimney, higher and narrower than the earlier one, gave me a twinge of worry. Good Lord, could it topple? I took added care to interlock stones, so that all joints were spanned by a stone of the next layer and were also overlapped by interior stones. When an awkward faceting of adjoining stones made it impossible for me to interlock them, I laced in baling wire or lengths of metal.

"Looks good, Zeke."

Finished, the chimney jutted above the roof, its straw-colored tiles poking up like smoke pipes of a French cottage. After the kids were in bed, Phyllis and I built a gentle fire. Seated on a split-log bench, watching the rose and amber flames do their lazy dance, I felt a great sense of peace—and weariness.

"Long have we toiled like peons," I said. "Sore has grown my back. Now we shall remove forty thalers from the Royal Treasury and go on a weekend trip."

Phyllis looked wistful, then shook her head. "Long have we toiled—true. Yet sorer still shall grow my back. For I, Queen of the Sticks, am pregnant again."

Hours after the house was asleep, I lay awake. Ice-coated branches clicked above the roof. I stared at the darkness over my bunk.

New life ... again.

Well, we wanted a family. We had heat, an extra crib—and a baby didn't eat much. One story, sold to a decent-paying magazine, would take care of it.

I went to the bathroom. In the mirror, I touched my chin. My hand was quivering very slightly. I balled it into a fist.

"You sick, honey?" said Phyllis, after I had climbed back into bed.

"No."

Her hand reached across in the dark and crumpled my hair.

"I saved all the baby stuff from Chris," she said.

"We'll be okay."

But something wasn't okay—with me. Whatever it was, I hugged it to myself. Somehow the effort to stay cheerful was growing harder.

One blustery night I drove into Bellows Falls. A beer can blew down a deserted street, winking. Colored lights, looping across Main Street, rocked wildly. All at once a string of them fell, exploding and blacking out.

At that moment I began thinking about friends who had died in the war. My roommate, Harry Stengle, shot down over Belgium. My football teammate, Bill Satterthwaite, killed on Okinawa.

Bouncing up our mountain, I tapped my fingers on the steering wheel. *Come on, man, look away from sadness. There's a whole life up ahead.*

Baby Girl on the Way
(It Says Here)

WINTER WAS BACK, but we were ready for it. Firewood was stacked under a big tar-paper lean-to. The oil tanks were full. The jeep had new plugs and points.

I put a Benny Goodman disc on our home-built record player and did a solo flea-hop in front of the fire.

The kids goggled. Phyllis said, "Is this a rain dance or a snow dance?"

"It's the Sister Stomp. It works on the unborn."

We would need powerful medicine to produce a girl in this family. I told Phyllis to stare at girl pictures in magazines and to stop wearing dungarees.

"The old boy is gone, Lord," she said, addressing the ceiling. "Send help."

For a surprise, heavy snow didn't come. The mountain wore a threadbare December shawl, which had a special beauty all its own. Morning after morning, mist from the pond and brook froze delicately on the trees. The Knoll glistened with tiny silver spikes. When we walked, the ground felt like knobby golf balls, rising and sinking.

We threw out crumbs for the birds, and they came in clouds. Chickadees, grackles, jays—even a flame-red cardinal. Animal life seemed to stir uneasily all around us, as if to ask, "Where's the snow?"

Without drifts to cover the lower part of the house, icy wind razored its way in. We covered sills and thresholds with towels and rugs. But we had to keep the fireplace going to stay comfortable. For a while, I found it more pleasant to spend off hours by the fire than to ramble around in the raw cold outside.

One evening, when Phyllis had taken Pete to the movies in Bellows Falls and Mike and Chris were in bed, I walked about the house, making a descriptive list. After all, I was supposed to be a writer, and this could pass as work, thus relieving my Puritan sense of guilt at three hours of idleness.

Among other things, I wrote:

Doorknob sticky with jam ... cat asleep, half in a toy-block garage ... lumps of wet clothes in a basket waiting to be hung out ... one carrot disk on the green linoleum kitchen floor ... dust swept in little piles, waiting to be picked up ... Xmas cards scotch-taped to the mantel . . . coat hanger bent, water-soaked coat in a heap beneath (the weight proved too much) ... squeezed orange halves, piled on each other like little hats ... cat's dish with rim of dried milk ... message clothespinned to bathroom curtain: "Turn off faucet hard." . . . eggbeater crusted with yellow, half-drowned in a frying pan of white fat ...

Then, just to keep in motion, I washed the dishes and picked up the rooms.

In the morning, Phyllis served breakfast. She said "Here's your orange juice—squeezed from halves piled on each other like little hats."

"Eh?"

"And here are your eggs—crusted with yellow, half-drowned in white fat."

"Ah," I said. "My notes . . ."

She waved them in front of me. "Your courtroom charges, you mean."

I looked down the list. "Well, there *are* a few items here a suspicious mind might call negative."

She said, "Dust swept in little piles, waiting to be picked up—that one really sends me."

"It has a ring."

"And," she said, pointing at the kitchen floor, "I've left that one carrot disk on the green linoleum, so you can admire it while you eat."

After breakfast, Phyllis worked at the sink. I put on my coat.

I said, "Toss me that dish sponge, will you?"

She looked around. "Sponge?"

"I want to wipe the jam off the doorknob."

Zap. I ducked in time, but the sodden sponge showered water on my face.

In the jeep I cranked down the window and shouted, "Don't forget to hang out those lumps of wet clothes."

She shook her fist. But as she turned away, I saw her eyes sparkle with mirth and her shoulders quake.

The snow came at last. It didn't amount to much, however. Winds soon swept the Knoll half-bare, and we could see yellow grass sticking up. Bitter cold set in—20-below . . . 30-below. The houses in Saxtons River, fed by springs, began to lose their water.

"Anything flowing on the mountain?" asked Bernie Clark, one of the town's overworked plumbers.

"We and the Bradleys are okay," I said.

Bernie rubbed his face. He was a handsome guy in his thirties with boundless energy. He had built his business from scratch, even laying the concrete blocks for his own shop while putting in rugged days plumbing. Now, for the first time, he was moving more slowly.

"I've been up all night," he said. "Half the lines in the streets are frozen. You can't find 'em—three houses here on a line, five houses there. Separate springs. This water system must have been pieced together before the Civil War."

His men were jackhammering through the glaciated asphalt. When they found a frozen pipe, they tried to thaw it electrically or with blowtorches. But the weather was not cooperating. "I've never seen a winter like this," said Bernie. "No snow cover, wind keeps blowing—and the thermometer has dropped through the bottom."

It was a brutal time—an Arctic paralysis. For weeks Bernie, Lefty Moore, and other experienced plumbers strove to keep a trickle of water moving, but homes everywhere went dry. Driving to Chester on the Grafton Road, I saw lines of trucks at the public spring and farmers filling milk cans.

"It's a good time to cut soft maples," Richard Bradley told me. "Five whacks of the ax and push. The tree falls over, and the frozen limbs break off."

The woods did seem as fragile as glass. Gradually ice grew over the branches. Many icicles, shaped just right, became prisms twinkling with red, yellow, and sapphire sunlight. When we walked through the woods, the ground was granite under our boots. And if we waded in a brook, thick platters of ice broke.

The time was agony for farmers. The line leading from Roland Aldrich's spring to his barn froze, and he had to haul water for about one hundred head of cattle. Ever resourceful, he strung a 1½-inch pipeline *over* the ground, letting it run continuously. But one frigid, windy night, even this free-flowing stream jammed. By morning it was a solid bar. Soon the metal began to split.

He bought 2-inch plastic pipe; but, by the time he and Hoppy took it off the truck, the coils were frozen. Each coil became a giant spring that would *boi-i-ing* back into a circle every time they tried to unwind it.

The Bradley and Morrill spreads, however, fed by spring lines that went through swamps, enjoyed a never-ending flow of water. It came out of the faucet like liquid frost, but it came. Since occasionally Richard and I had endured jibes at our outback life-style, it was hard not to be smug. We were careful, however, to keep our faces tragic when discussing the water problem with village folk.

By Christmas we were living in a silver-glazed wonderland. The windows were completely sheeted with ice. Sunlight, glinting through them, rippled like an amber-and-pink river. We had to push Duke and the cats out of the house each day. They ran around with smoky puffs at their mouths, and in minutes they scratched at the door for reentry.

The kids got new sleds as presents. But the Knoll, wearing only a skim of snow, didn't encourage sliding. Mike and Chris tried anyway, but were soon back, shivering.

"Look," said Chris, red-faced, holding up his tiny wrist where he had sucked the wool of his jacket. The wetness had frozen into a dollar-sized wafer. "I can make ice."

In late January snow arrived—quite a lot of it. But the weather took another freakish swerve, and everything melted. The jeep ground through prairies of slush. At the post office, neighbors cussed the skies, the roads—and the government for good measure.

Still, there were sudden bright moments—real intrusions of beauty. And these continued to make mountain life a joy.

One morning in February we awoke to find the whole visible world sheathed in ice. All night long there had been a freezing rain. The forest had groaned and cracked beneath it's weight, and big limbs hung broken. I stepped outside into brilliant sunlight. Instantly my feet flew out from under me. Sprawled on the mirrorlike stone step, I ran my hand over the muddy turf. It was hard . . . slippery.

"Hey! Everything's glass!"

A transparent coat lay on every square inch. To get up, I had to reach across the threshold and pull myself into the house.

"Getting to school will be a ball," said Phyllis.

Heavier these days, she still loved running the Saxtons River Kindergarten in its big, new room. All winter she had not missed a day. Jeanette lived with us now in the ell, so we didn't have to worry about a baby-sitter. Since Vermont schools stayed open in the worst weather (in contrast to Connecticut, where a two-inch snow-dusting might cause a shutdown), Phyllis was determined to get to her desk.

We slithered to the jeep. Creeping in low-range, four-wheel drive, I ventured out our gate. The jeep turned sideways and glided into the ditch.

We got out—and immediately sprawled.

"Look, the road's *in armor*," said Phyllis.

The gravel was enameled with ice. Sitting there, we slid our palms over a surface that looked rough but that a centipede could not have stood up on.

Our friendly old dirt road had become a silver scimitar glittering toward the Bradleys'. A pink sun blazed in a heron-blue heaven. The whole world seemed to be an Arabian fantasyland.

We pushed with our hands—and sailed. This way. That way. We wound up in the ditch, tangled together. Phyllis stretched out on her back and shoved herself into the road.

"Wheeeeeeeeeeeeeeeeee!"

Round and round she went, looking up at the sky. I tried it and finished far down the ditch.

It was childhood all over again. Icy surface on our backs. Whirling clouds. Push by push, we rode this giant playground slide a mile or more toward town.

When Roland Aldrich rescued us in his chain-wheeled pickup, we were cold and wet. But Phyllis squeezed my hand and whispered, "That was *beautiful*."

Again, we were hit head on by the beauty of northern lights. One night, when a frosting of snow had returned to the mountain, we were awakened by light rippling through the window. We got out of our bunks. Green-and-crystal tints revolved on the floor. We got dressed and went to the Knoll.

As far as we could see, the snowy hills were undulating. We stood in the center of monster seas that moved but didn't move. The whole sky was curiously liquid, and it made the distant Saxtons River steeples waver like flames. We felt tiny, but safe in the universe.

So spring slushed in once more. Duke jackknifed up Little Baldy and returned with his tongue out and his flanks muddy—*à la* Feather. Tumbling water laced the mountain. We heard the brook *glug-glugging* night and day.

We had made it through another winter, easy as pie. But, again, we were startled by how swiftly Time was flowing. Five years we had lived on the mountain, and it still seemed that we had just arrived. Meanwhile, the world was racing ahead. The Korean War had come and gone. Stalin had died. But the evening news still crackled with rumors of fresh fights and grim prospects.

"Maybe it's not the best time to bring new life into

173

the world," said Phyllis. "But we've got the best place to do it, anyhow."

"And a girl will soften up things around here," I said.

Our orbit was almost totally masculine. Phyllis was forever picking up boxing gloves and baseballs, hammers and homemade hockey sticks. I knew she mused wistfully about spreading a tiny skirt on the ironing board amid the shirts and pants.

One Saturday the boys and I had a snowball fight—or rather, snow*mush* fight—on the thawing Flat. It wound up with all of us soaked and shivering. We took hot showers. Phyllis opened a new package of towels, just arrived from New York. (We always indulged ourselves with "seconds" of the biggest and thickest towels from Macy's, for there's nothing that lifts the morale like drying yourself with luxuriant cotton on a cold day.)

Jeanette was away, so the four of us stood naked in front of a roaring fire. We sawed our backs with the big red towels. We pranced around, reviewing the fight.

Phyllis looked. "Oh," she said and fled to the bedroom.

Later, when I came in, she was reading a *McCall's*. She said, "I'm staring at every girl on the page for thirty seconds."

On a wet night I skied along the slushy Knoll. I stopped and lifted both ski poles at some stars made dim by mist. Time seemed to *rush* by, the way calendar leaves go fluttering across a screen in an old Hollywood sequence. Hundreds of years whished past, and our cabin—glowing fuzzily through the birches—was blotted out. Where the two chimneys had jutted, only mounds remained. Woods rose around me. Monster oaks and weird vines covered the road. Not the slightest mark remained to hint that a long-vanished family had worked out a dream here. . . .

This is how it will actually be someday.

Suddenly my stomach felt like lead. I rammed my poles into the slush. I shot recklessly for a strip of shadow alongside Pete's Pool. Hissing down the watery surface, my skis aimed at a narrow gap between trees and brook.

WHAM. Everything blazed white.

I woke up shivering. I was sprawled on the other side of Pete's Pool, soaked through. I got up gingerly, feeling for broken bones. There were none, but my right ski was snapped off just below the toe, and I could find only one pole.

"Honey, what did you *do*?"

Phyllis daubed my bleeding forehead. I peeled off my wet clothes. The kids came to stare at me wonderingly, their faded Dr. Denton pajamas flapping at the toes.

"I was racing to catch my lost youth," I said.

"Did you catch it?"

I shook my head. "Another time."

She wiped my head with a towel. "You want me to grow old by myself?"

The kids went back to bed. The night sounds floated back—the toilet flushing, a radio announcer saying: "Cloudy tonight, rain tomorrow . . ."

From the bedroom Mike's voice piped up:

> Peter is a friend of mine.
> He's as fat as Frankenstein.
> When he walks on down the street.
> You can smell his stinky feet.

And then a gale of laughter.

Neighbors and Things

Just as spring, 1956, arrived, something abnormal happened. The final snowstorm of the season came—a jolt back to midwinter. The temperature dropped to 15-above. An eight-inch layer fell, powder-soft.

Unexpectedly, the jeep radiator broke and spurted purple antifreeze over the white spread. For the first time, Phyllis missed school. I called to tell Readex not to expect me.

"Twenty-four hours of total holiday," I said.

The kids ran out with their sleds. Phyllis, Jeanette, and I waded through drifts, zippered to the nose.

"Everything's crazy-white," said Jeanette, smacking her mittens together. "This is wild."

Although a radiant sun shone, the winds were rising. The woods *smoked.* Great swirls of snow blew off the evergreens, spiraled up, and became gauzy clouds. It was a sifty, sugary world. It blinded the eyes and stung the face.

"Shout!" cried Phyllis.

We shouted. The kids' heads popped up like chipmunks from behind a drift.

176

"It's all right. We're just having fun."

We got shovels and started to dig a path, but it was hopeless. The shovelfuls blew apart as we lifted them. We went sliding instead. Phyllis, trying to be careful, took rides only on the smaller slope toward the Bradleys'. Jeanette, Pete, Mike, Chris, and I rode the back-busting roller west of the Knoll.

Sometime before noon, Roland Aldrich's tractor chugged up the road, its chains slapping.

"Plow truck is broken," he said. "You're locked in."

He stayed for hot chocolate, then offered to bring groceries. But we needed nothing.

"You're sure tucked in here nice," he said admiringly.

For the rest of the day we frolicked at the core of a season that we had thought was over. It gave us a droll sense of time lag. In the afternoon I worked on the jeep radiator, scraping a snow trough to lie in. Once something small and wet blew against my cheek. I scraped it off. It was a tender green birch leaf, born too soon.

"Tomorrow," exulted Pete, "we're gonna build two snow forts and have a war."

We went to bed with windows open only a crack and cold air chiseling our covers. Vermont had played another of her climatic tricks. Geared for spring, we had reverted to little figures in a Currier & Ives print labeled "Winter in the Woods."

But in the night we woke to hear snow sliding off the roof. Rain fell. The storm grew to a thunderous, house-shaking downpour. By dawn the mountain was bare. Unbelievably, six hours of thaw had erased our polar wonderland like a wet rag sloshed across a chalkboard.

"The thermometer has risen from fifteen to sixty-five," said Phyllis. "How's that for Instant Climate Control?"

I got the jeep back onto the road. For a couple of days I labored through quagmires. Then the ruts dried out, and the fumy warmth of May took over. Even before our mittens and sweaters were put away, insects began bumping against our lighted lamppost.

At the bottom of the hill, between the Aldrich and Barnes farms, lived Norman Benware, and this spring more log trucks than usual pulled up at his place on Saturday nights. Norman was a sawyer. He worked in surrounding mills. He and his sons were in a hard business, and weekends brought welcome relief—visitors. Around suppertime his slanty yard filled up with unshaven men, tired wives, dogs, and geese. The men saluted us with beer cans as we passed.

Norman's wife worked in the Rockingham Hospital. Despite babies of her own, hard hours, and little money, she held the show together. Year by year as we had been hard-slogging it on the mountain, we had watched them hard-slogging it down below. And I had noticed steady changes in their battle to survive. The faded tar-paper siding on their house gave way to clapboards. Flowers popped up along the porch. The sons built a handsome stone retaining wall on one side and created a lush lawn there.

One night my car quit near the house, and Norman came out to help. He held a flashlight while I taped up a leaky heater hose.

"Never seen machinery yet that wouldn't slap a man down when he least needs it," he said.

We got water from his kitchen. I noticed that, like us, the Benwares were remodeling and re-remodeling. A new sink and refrigerator were in. And the small living room had fresh ceiling squares.

"Takes time," said Norman, waving his gnarled hand half apologetically.

We got the car going. Meanwhile, Norman and I

had shaken our heads over the condition of the road and had griped about how taxes kept rising.

"Getting me a saw rig of my own," he said. "Gonna take a hell of a time to pay for it, but it don't make sense to work for wages these days."

In time he was to do just that. He bought a used rig—heavy engine, table-sized blade, and sliding gear to handle giant logs. He set it up beside his house. When a disgruntled villager complained about the noise and tried to halt the operation by pointing out that Norman didn't own enough acres to make it legal, neighbor Barnes came through with the needed land.

Shortly, log trucks arrived—great, snorting vehicles with crumpled fenders and tall loads. The logs rolled onto the platform. The Benware sons, skilled and muscular, clamped them into position. The big blade screamed. Hour after hour the logs moved. Slices of marble-colored hemlock slid off into piles. Norman presided at the main lever, his bushy beard flying in the breeze.

Bought in painful installments, the sawmill proved a point—that a tenacious Vermont family could hang in there and build a business in the country in this age. The sawmill's bright aluminum roof proclaimed success along Hartley Hill Road—something to cleave to in our minds.

Before we knew it, the heat-stunned days were on us. I drove to work with clouds of dust billowing from the jeep wheels. School was finished, Jeanette gone to get married. Phyllis, uncomfortable in her bulky maternity dress, labored through the housework, then sat under a tree on the Flat. I usually found her lost in a book, while changing position every two minutes on the chaise.

"This baby is a kicker," she said, holding her side.

"It's good to have a kicking girl amidst brothers," I said.

For several weeks each day seemed the same—carved from pearl. Red sun. Motionless leaves. Droning bees. All vegetation grew at high speed. Driving to Chester, I saw houses that had stood starkly alone through the winter now sinking in green seas, like hulls of ships.

But, if the days were all hotness and honeysuckle, the nights were pure sorcery. The twilight tinsel on trees changed from scarlet to purple. The steamy earth grew cool. Each night we walked to the Knoll and watched ermine clouds do slow dervish dances over Saxtons River.

"People must be suffering in the cities," I said. "Thank God for *space*."

It made up for the rough winter—this soft-candled sky of June did. The valley had an ageless peace, lighted by the silent flashes of fireflies.

"Thank God for the pond, too," said Phyllis.

The pond was getting a workout. Young swimmers were showing up from all over. One afternoon the entire Saxtons River baseball team plunged in. Mike and I built a raft, nailing a frame around some empty two-gallon oil cans. On still evenings, he rode amid dipping barn swallows, his paddle making circles on the pink flesh of the water.

The best part of this hot interlude, I discovered, was coming home and finding new kids splashing where there had once been only deserted swamp. It gave me a sense of having built something useful and permanent. And the sound of *girls'* voices—so light, so different—fell quaintly on the ear.

One lavender sundown I sat alone by the garage and listened to cries and splashes from the pond. Feminine laughter drifted through the birches, and it filled me with young dreams. A breeze stirred. High overhead the trees shivered, and something nudged me to get up and climb Big Baldy.

I climbed through thickening twilight. Leaves rustled. A breeze was rising, the first in days. Lexie and Prince neighed and eyed me suspiciously as I jumped the Bradleys' barbed-wire fence. Near the top of Big Baldy, I found a giant, lightning-scarred oak. I stepped on a burl, heaved myself into a wide crotch, and started working upward through monstrous branches.

At twenty feet I felt the tree move thickly. At thirty feet its sway grew stronger. At forty feet the trunk became a mast—and I was back at sea, reeling in the wind.

Minutes passed. Beyond an orange layer of hills, I could see a storm coming this way. It moved swiftly. A sound like paper tearing floated from the forest. The leaves turned up white undersides, and I felt a throb of excitement. I was aboard a tossing ship again!

I clung there, remembering. I rocked over the surging ocean of Vermont. Far below, voices drifted from the pond, indistinguishable. Our house roof, looking very small, jutted through the trees. There lay my homestead—my castle with Queen, three Princes, and three-quarters of a Princess.

A thought, unexpected and mocking, flashed through my mind: *If you had stayed at sea, you'd have been a captain by now—with your own command.*

I hung in the oak, brooding. Then dragons of lightning flashed above the Grafton Road. The kids fled the pond. Thunder rumbled. Suddenly the house looked very good—a brave little stockade in the darkening wilderness.

I scrambled down. I reached our screen door just as the first raindrops splattered.

The morning was fresh-washed and cool. Since it was Saturday, I waited until after breakfast to drive down for the mail. I turned across the Dows' big stone culvert, and a scrawny little figure in the road waved me to a halt.

"Next week my raspberries will be ready," the figure said. "I'll leave your box in the barn—same as always."

It was Ernie Dow, the old man who lived in a paint-peeling house between the Bradleys' and the Aldriches'. He wore sneakers, striped underwear shorts, red suspenders—and nothing else. He was bent and rickety, but the skin of his naked torso was like hard brown leather.

"Okay, Mr. Dow," I half shouted.

"Get out. I want to show you."

I followed him into his raspberry field. Now and then he turned to see if I was following (he was almost totally deaf). His eyes searched me, blue and innocent as a child's.

"Now see here, Morrill, I've put pipes from here to the brook. Water comes in gravity feed."

"I see."

"The drier the weather gets, the better I like it."

"Very good."

We had gone through this routine several times. But Ernie was forgetful, or he was so proud of his system he couldn't help showing it again and again. The perforated pipes, shoulder high, sprayed water on his thick raspberry bushes. He raised berries that were the wonder of the county—fat, red, and indescribably tasty. He charged 50 cents for a heaping quart box.

"I've been here a good many years."

"I know you have."

In fact, the old man was living in the same house he had been born in. Everything about the place bespoke the long ago. Firewood, covered with dust, was stacked in a shed, ready for stoves no longer used. A phonograph, with cylindrical records, sat in the living room. There was an old sleigh in the barn, and Ernie kept a buffalo robe in the loft to nap on.

Ernie's wife was a stooped old woman who had been his housekeeper. She walked painfully, and continually dabbed a handkerchief at her face, where a cancer, which she refused to have treated, was eating the flesh. Every day the mail carrier drove her to Bellows Falls, and she walked the streets, looking at people. She came back with the afternoon mail.

Her whole life was making that trip—and listening over the telephone. She would sit by the window, her hand on the receiver. Whenever there was a faint click on our party line, she would lift the receiver noiselessly and tune in on what was happening. Her lifting technique was superb, but her listening skill was faulty—she leaned so close to the mouthpiece that everyone could hear her rasping breath.

This eavesdropping could be annoying, particularly when we were trying to hear a long-distance call over our creaky system. Mrs. Dow's breathing befogged the voices. Roland Aldrich, who did cattle business at long range, finally installed a private system. Richard Bradley, who was fond of the prickly old woman, would shout jovially: "All right down there—get off the line. I'm talking to Medford." My *modus operandi* was to say, "Mrs. Dow, this is a long-distance call, and I can't hear it. Would you hang up for a few minutes?"

Mrs. Dow's breathing would stop. *Crash*, down would go the receiver.

"My wife spends her time in the house and in Bellows Falls," Ernie said, handing me a raspberry. "I spend mine out here. I like it that way."

He walked back to the house, bent like a gnome, his fluffy, bleached hair shaking with each step. As I climbed into my jeep, he looked up and waved a bony hand. He was the Little Old Man of the Mountain, his sunbrowned body afloat in suspenders and underwear shorts. A true creature of the raspberry patch.

"Don't forget to stop for your box every night," he said, nibbling on a berry.

I drove off, feeling as if I had just talked with a timeless Peter Rabbit. I had no inkling of the tragedy that would eventually overtake him.

Downtown I ran into Chuck Blakney and we talked about the Church Problem. The Church Problem was insoluble. It stemmed from the fact that there were two big Protestant buildings in town, and neither had a congregation large enough to support it. One, Congregationalist, had the best location in town, at the head of Main Street. The other, Baptist, had the superior structure, towering over Fuller Hardware. The sects had already combined in a Federated Church, but they could not agree on which church to abandon. So they met six months in one, six months in the other—and struggled to keep both buildings shingled, painted, and repaired.

"In the old days the church dominated everyone's time and money," said Chuck. "Now the town can't handle two big plants like that."

In fact, he went on, Saxtons River suffered from *too many* large meeting places. Besides the churches, it had the grammar school, the Odd Fellows Hall, Kurn Hattin auditorium, and Vermont Academy.

"It's inevitable that some of them will fall off," he said. "Look what's happening to the Old South Meeting House."

"That's the most beautiful building in town," I protested.

He shrugged. "Sure—but it's going."

The Old South Meeting House was a graceful clapboard structure built in the early 1800s. It had once boasted a high cupola. Handsome Doric columns rose on either side of its stately front door, but they were beginning to lose their wooden fluting. Massive hand-hewn timbers showed through. The roof leaked.

"Tenney's beginning to store lumber in there now," said Chuck.

"What!"

It was true. Trucks pulled up under arching trees that had seen Civil War volunteers assemble. Men piled ceiling board on floors where long-vanished townsmen had spoken out. The Old South Meeting House, standing proudly at the entrance to the town cemetery, was on the way to oblivion.

"Can't the town save it?" I asked Humphrey Neill.

"The people can't get together," he said. "The deed is cloudy, you know. The place was used as a school for some time. Then the Sons of Union Veterans got hold of it. We'd have to get the heirs of every SUV member to sign for a clear title. They're spread all over the country now."

"How did Tenney get it?"

"He got it on a quitclaim deed."

"Nobody challenged it?"

"Nobody can find a better claim."

I talked with Tenney at the lumber mill. "Actually," he said, "I've saved the building. I've patched the roof, timbered up the floors."

I got the impression that his was a holding operation until the village decided what it wanted to do. Meanwhile, the place belonged to him and he was going to use it profitably.

With Tenney's permission, I explored the old building. Broken glass and splinters littered the floor. I climbed into the belfry, stepping gingerly on boards worn by generations of feet. Some startled birds flew out of gaping holes in the big side vents.

Wow!

There, crusted over with pigeon dung, stood a massive hand-hewn cradle. In the cradle hung a big bronze bell. I rubbed the side of the bell. Slowly the words came to view: *Revere—Boston.*

I climbed down, thinking what great effort must have been expended to erect so noble an edifice. In the energetic youth of the Republic, such an outpouring of community sacrifice had really meant something.

And how would the ghosts of those builders look on a later generation that was letting the Old South Meeting House die?

I drove home, a bit depressed. But a few hundred yards this side of my gate I heard the bang-bang of a hammer. My car pulled over the rise, and there was Richard Bradley on the rafters of his new house, slamming away. His gray hair bounced with each swing. He leaned down and shouted to Si Finch for another plank. . . .

Up. Down. That's how my moods went. Richard Bradley's vigor was like a bottled spirit. I sipped of it whenever I was feeling low. I never knew whether he suspected the roller coaster I was secretly riding, but one time he talked about the healing nature of labor.

"About twenty years ago a carpenter feller come up here feeling bad," he said. "Asked me if he could camp out on Big Baldy until he died."

The carpenter's wife had run away, and he was sick of living. Richard told him to set up his tent. For a week the man stayed out of sight, only a thread of smoke marking the site of his camp.

"We was building my horse barn at the time, and you could hear our hammers all over Windham County. Bangity-bang. Pretty soon the feller comes

186

down the mountain. He looks at our job and says we're doing it all wrong. He picks up a hammer...."

Richard chuckled. The carpenter had pitched in, day after day. As the barn went up, his cheeks grew tan and muscles hard again.

"He's living in Bellows Falls right now. Comes up and sees me once in a while—he and his new wife."

The gospel of work. There was something to it, all right. While Phyllis went humming about her duties, I sweated and swore over the typewriter. Then, dizzy with words and half blind from poring over my checkbook, I seized an ax and slaved to exhaustion in the woods.

I fortified myself with axioms gleaned from hither and yon: "Sorrow is the mere rust of the soul. Activity will cleanse and brighten it."—Sam Johnson

And I frolicked with my small sons, alternating between the roles of clown and worried breadwinner.

But even work cannot halt the bitter chemistry of depression. I wrote to an old schoolteacher friend, peeling back slightly the curtain that covered my heart, "Why this damned ghost of futility hovering about? I'm doing exactly what I always wanted up here."

He wrote back that I was "wearing the Nessus shirt," a garment of torture that all thinking people donned once in a while no matter how they directed their lives. His message reinforced my own stubborn belief: Hang in there; the change will come.

The change came. It was not, however, for the better. I read a true account of a World War I flier, a hero who had triumphed over plane wrecks, wounds, and terror. After conquering all meaningful obstacles, he had lost some money in the stock market—and shot himself.

"He couldn't face a *new* adversary," I observed to

Phyllis. "He could take physical pain and danger. But bankruptcy—a slithery, subtle thing—"

"Maybe he didn't have love."

"I wonder what it feels like to go broke. Flat out. Finished."

She grinned. "You know, we could make a habit of blowing out the light to see how dark it is. Now what if a tree falls on the house . . . ?"

So I slogged on, puzzled. I forced myself to take an interest in everything. And, gradually, I felt new sympathy—and admiration—for a suffering world. *Any sort of pain*, I wrote, *even self-induced as I believe mine is, should make a man more tolerant of others' troubles. But he musn't become a tearjerk, sloshing unwanted compassion on everybody. His mind must grow tougher as his hand grows gentler.*

One day at Readex I jammed my finger in the press and gouged it to the bone. While getting it stitched at the Chester Clinic, I hesitantly broached my perplexity to Doc Griffith, the understanding country physician who had delivered Christopher. He nodded. "Fatigue, melancholy, so on, eh? Sounds like EII."

"What's that?"

"Emotion Induced Illness. How much time off you get up on that mountain?"

"Well, I write on weekends, build on holidays—but that's really a kind of recreation too."

He looked at me. "Work is great. Too much is like alcohol—it depresses you. How much Boni paying you?"

"Eighty-five a week."

"Can you live on that?"

"We're still eating."

He rubbed his face wearily. "Emotion Induced Illness. I get it too. I wonder if my kid is blowing her chances at college. I wonder if we're going broke with

188

this clinic. There's never enough money or time for what a man wants to do."

I turned toward the door, my bandaged finger beginning to throb.

Doc smiled. "I guess the secret is to slow down—if you can. And wait. Country life knocks you out if you fight it, but picks you up again if you slack off."

That night I tramped through woods behind the cabin and wondered about the men who had broken their lives building the stone walls I climbed.

Relax, I told myself, *but keep busy. Don't slave for money, but don't run out of it. Think, but don't worry. How in hell does a guy find the formula?*

At bedtime Phyllis said, "You know, you're more interesting than you were as a hotshot sailor. You're getting little crinkles around the eyes."

Here We Go Again

"I FEEL," said Phyllis, looking at herself in the mirror, "like a watermelon with knitting needles for legs."

I dissented. "More the balloon type. Roundish . . ."

"So? I can *roll* to the auction."

Richard Bradley was selling out, getting ready to move into his personally built Cape Cod house. The new building, when finished, would jut from a hillock 100 yards below our Knoll. It was much smaller than his big, old farmhouse, so he would have to unload a lot of his furnishings.

I helped him line up his farm equipment in the pasture: horse-drawn mowing machine, manure spreader, cream separator, rakes, plows—a lifetime accumulation of things needed to wrench a livelihood from the Vermont soil. In his attic we found ancient bureaus, guns, and clothes. It all came downstairs, ready to be hauled up onto the block—including a battered bugle used for years to call hayers from the fields at dinnertime. (In the end the bugle was not sold, sentiment triumphing over economics.)

Meantime, Si pushed feed at the cattle to fill them

out for the buyers. He cleaned the stalls in the big barn. He mowed around the horse barn and milkhouse. He slapped a fresh coat of red paint on the chicken shed. By the morning of the auction the Bradleys' farm gleamed.

We rose early. Pete and Mike were so excited at breakfast that they couldn't eat. We gave each kid twenty-five cents for a soda and hot dog at the refreshment table. By nine o'clock trucks with cattle trailers were grinding into the Bradleys' pasture. The auctioneer, an apple-cheeked man in a derby, was setting up his amplifier. Vermont farm folk—old men with canes, women with red hands, children wearing threadbare sneakers—greeted each other.

It was odd to see strangers wandering through the Bradleys' barn, their eyes taking in everything. They joked with Richard. They picked up tools and set them down. Their wives fondled lamps and tried bureau drawers.

The amplifier crackled. "Well, folks, ain't this a likely day to git yourself a bargain or three . . ."

The auction swung to life. Si led heifers into a circle. Farmers touched them with their canes and considered them through squinted eyes.

"Yessir, there's a fine animal. Now, who'll give me two hundred . . . ?"

Within half an hour it was evident that Richard had picked the right time to sell. Prices were up. Bidders shook their heads and cursed softly, but they kept bidding.

"You're gonna have a pile, Richard," said one wrinkled old farmer.

"Not likely," Richard replied, but he looked pleased.

Friends of the Bradleys had added things to the auction, a customary procedure when a farm was selling out. Here was a battered bread mixer with crank, there a brass supper bell. Someone was putting up a big wheel-grindstone with rusty pedals and a bicycle seat. Amid the washing tubs and rolled-up rugs sat a forlorn baby carriage, its rattan sides cracked, its wheels atilt.

Voices drifted by: "I remember when your grandmother set up housekeeping down the Putney road. . . ."

". . . got in two hundred bales and, Jesus, how the rain come!"

". . . tother way. Past the Fisher farm. Trout fat as your arm."

". . . Gone. Jake's place too. Ned's sick and they're gonna sell."

In the ebb and flow, we caught the echo of old times and old places. And the stream of worn furnishings kept moving off the lawn onto pickups and car roofs.

"One fifty-four . . . Who'll give one fifty-five? *Five*, that gentleman in the white cap. Who'll go six . . . one fifty-six . . . ?"

By noon, half the substance of the farm was gone. The auctioneer droned on. I helped Si haul things around. I moved hay with a pitchfork. Phyllis sat uncomfortably on the porch steps and sipped coffee from a paper cup. "At two I'll take the kids home," she said. I tossed her the jeep keys.

Late in the afternoon the action dwindled. Trucks pulled out. Cattle bawled. A small knot of men followed the auctioneer through the pasture, bidding on the horse-drawn machinery, which didn't go for much. A few pieces didn't sell at all.

By suppertime the farm, which had been a going operation only hours before, was a scooped-out shell. I walked through the empty barn. The rich odors of bedding and manure still floated up, but all noise, all activity had vanished. Richard had made the money he wanted. Goods had been distributed sensibly. Farm people had renewed traditional ties.

Yet a sort of sadness drifted through the silent mow with its hand-hewn beams. This was the end of an era. Soon Lexie and Prince would be sold. Horse farming was leaving Hartley Hill for good.

The next day Richard dropped up, wearing a clean white shirt and bow tie. "I came to pay you for helping," he said.

"Are you kidding? I got a kick out of it."

"Well," he said, "that old slate sink we hauled up in the pasture didn't go. You take it—if you've a mind to."

I took it. Broken apart, the ancient, ugly sink made handsome bluish flags at our front door. Walking over them, I could remember the old farm.

About then we had other indications of passing time.

One Sunday Chuck Blakney announced to a startled congregation that he, his wife, and two children were going to Africa. "That's where the battleground of faith will be tomorrow," he said.

Before leaving, his wife gave us a playpen for the new baby. Chuck honked the horn as their old station wagon chugged out our gate for the last time, and we waved.

The grocery store changed hands. A big barn near Tenney's Lumber Mill burned. The town bought a new grader.

Even our pond was changing, maturing. From the start, people had insisted that we ought to fill it with trout. Dutifully, I signed up with a government agency to stock the place with fingerlings. Nothing happened. After a while, friends appeared with buckets of small trout caught (illegally) in surrounding streams. In the shiny wigglers went, *splash*—and were never seen again.

"Some sonsabitches are fishing 'em out at night," a friend told me.

I shrugged.

"Why dontcha start some underwater growth to feed fish?" he said.

I bought a bag of fertilizer and sprinkled it over the water. The growth came—wavy streamers that tickled our toes as we swam. But the fish did not.

"They hide, you know," said a fisherman wisely. "They hang around the bottom. I know how to reach 'em."

He—and others—tried this pole and that pole, this hook and that hook. They never caught anything. Then one day a fat, eighteen-inch trout floated up dead, and there was a new burst of enthusiasm.

"Je-zus!"

"Someone must have hooked that baby and lost her. Look, ain't that a scar on her mouth?"

"She died of old age. We were using the wrong hook."

"This pond is gonna have *millions* of fish."

The boys threw out their lines again. Every time a frog made a splash, they pointed and said, see, the trout were feeding. But no one pulled out a single fish. I decided that somebody had tossed in the dead trout for laughs.

I was careful, however, not to say so. And as the no-fish seasons stretched on, I nodded understandingly at the earnest theories that sprang up: the water was too cold or too hot . . . there wasn't enough shade . . . the fish had found something to eat on the bottom and had stayed there. . . .

At last we grew annoyed at the underwater growth; it slithered along our legs. I asked a biologist friend what to do about it.

"You can pour in chemicals," he said. "They'll kill the vegetation, but they'll halt your pond cycle too."

Nothing doing. We wanted more life, not less, in there.

"I've got some barbed wire," I said. "Maybe we can scrape the bottom—"

We attached double lengths of wire, considerably longer than the width of the pond, to hardwood handles. We bolted heavy objects (cast-iron pipe, gears, old car parts) at intervals along the lengths. With two people on each side of the pond pulling the handles. I guided the weighted wire into the water. We hauled a mass of weed to the end of the pond and raked it into a pile.

After two or three rakings, we had a heap of soggy vegetation—frogbit and mare's tail, flowering rush and smartweed. Tadpoles came up, squirming. Water bugs jumped. The whole mess reeked with primal energy.

We spread the stuff for fertilizer. And, after the pond mud had settled, we had clear swimming again.

As June deepened, I spent as much time as I could in the pond. One Sunday I worked my air mattress into the reeds and cattails at the north end. I drifted noiselessly into a world of slender arches and tangles—an entirely new setting for me. Lying still, I was visited by strange friends. Darning needles the color of grapes hovered an inch from my face. Water striders zipped by, their tiny legs flashing like oars. A frog landed on my back—plop—and jumped off again.

The sun was hot. But in my emerald wicker-house only soft yellow filtered through. I dozed, my feet trailing in the water. When I came to, teensy things were nibbling my toes. I opened an eye, and there, on the corner of my mattress, sat a blue frog.

He wasn't green-blue; he was *bright* blue, like wild lupine. We stared at each other, and I fixed his color in my mind. Yes, he was blue all right. Then another frog hopped up across from him. He was *turquoise*.

What was this? I had never seen technicolor frogs before. Father and son, maybe? After a while they left, and I was treated to another spectacle of frogdom: a battle to the death.

Two big bullfrogs swam around the end of the mattress. They met head on like brutal green wrestlers. They bit each other. They twisted each other's knobby arms. The fight ended with one frog floating helplessly, white belly to the sun, his throat bleeding.

Drifting out of the reeds, I mused on the variety of life that pulsated around this one dipperful of water. Our little pond was attracting everything from salamanders to passing ducks. It had truly transformed our property. Each season gave it a different image.

In summer it was a bowl of life-broth. In fall it became a blue mirror held up to racing clouds—a thing of thrills and luster. Winter changed it to a skillet of glass (at least until the first snowfall). And in spring it became a promise of life's renewal, so pure one could drink from it.

Toying with such thoughts, I paddled leisurely to the center. The kids had appeared, jumping off the stone dock. Phyllis waded along the tiny beach, her wide-brimmed hat cocked back. Duke came sniffing down the bank. What a lure was this pond—what a solace!

"Ho, every one that thirsteth," said Isaiah, "come ye to the waters."

I had need of solace. Affairs at Readex were in a new turmoil. The forelady had been absent five weeks for an operation, and her temporary replacement was doing a better job with film matters concerning New York.

Albert Boni called. "I want you to let the old forelady go."

I swallowed—audibly.

"Now don't worry about this. I have to do this all the time," he went on.

I said nothing. I knew that Albert shrank from firing anyone himself and was relishing the distance between us.

"Do that right away."

I sat in the forelady's small living room. She was a divorcée with a young daughter. She looked wan and stunned, but she didn't break down.

"As soon as you're gone, I'll probably bawl," she said.

That night I told Phyllis I wished I were in the word business full time, as an editor or something.

"At heart I'm a lone putterer," I said. "I like to fiddle around with tools and ideas."

"At heart you're a fiction writer," she said.

"And fiction is dying in the magazines. I should have been writing in the twenties and thirties."

"You could go back to teaching. In that biz, we're *all* putterers."

I reflected on the idea. I got as far as talking with the headmasters at Vermont Academy and Deerfield. But always I found myself back behind the typewriter in my packing-crate office. I was happiest honing paragraphs—or swinging a hammer.

It was now midsummer. The July sounds—the *scr-r-itch* of a cat on the screen door, the *ka-knock-knock* of a woodpecker—were muted by thick foliage overhanging the house. Most of the time we had blanching heat, and Phyllis suffered. But sometimes great whacking winds came down at night. Then we would walk to the Knoll, open our clothes, and let the coolness lave us.

"I've decided on a name for this baby—Holly," said Phyllis.

I rolled it on my tongue approvingly. A moment later I said, "And I've got her middle name—Hock."

She looked at me. "Well, so much for Holly Hock Morrill. How about Beth?"

We settled tentatively on Beth Ann.

While troubled over Readex, I found relief in building a tree hut with the kids. Chris hauled bottles of drinking water in his little red wagon as Pete, Mike, and I pounded beams in a big beech tree. We built the platform twenty feet up.

Halfway through, we ran out of scrap lumber. "They're tearing down a house in Bellows Falls," said Pete hopefully. "Maybe they'll sell some."

The boys counted out their pennies. We stopped at the half-demolished building. The head wrecker, a friendly, sweat-streaked man with only one (very powerful) arm, took in the situation at a glance.

"Take what you need," he said. "Two bucks."

We got three loads of splintered planks and two-by-fours. It took a solid day of nail pulling and scraping to clean the plastery wood, but at last we had enough to build a room that could sleep two adults or three kids. It had a waterproof tar-paper roof. It had a trapdoor leading to ladder steps nailed up the trunk.

"KEEP OUT. BEWARE," Mike painted on the side. He added a blotchy skull and crossbones.

Another diversion helped me forget Chester: working in my field. I loafed along with my scythe, trying to ignore the sardonic glances of Shorty, Bean Pole, and Hercules.

One Saturday afternoon I mowed awhile, then lay down in the shade of a maple and fell asleep. When the sun shifted, I awoke. My eye focused foggily on a weird monster from Mars—crazy-legged, grotesque—climbing a green pole. I blinked at it. The monster turned out to be an ant going up a grass stalk an inch from my nose.

Something made a movement, and I rolled my eyes sideways. Four feet away sat a bobolink nest. Three heads—like tiny walnuts—bobbed silently. The mother bird crouched nearby, its bronze-streaked body motionless. All the time they had made no sound, even as my scythe swished near and I had flopped down.

"Wildlife handle tension better than we do," I told Phyllis.

"Your ol' field talking to you again, Zeke?"

That was about the size of it. As Phyllis entered her final restless week, a pleasant calm came over me. From now on, I would crouch motionless beside the unknowns of childbirth and career—and simply wait for time to pass.

In mid-July the baby watch ended. Phyllis snapped on the light over her bunk.

"Beth, you sure picked the time," she said.

"I'll alert Pete," I said.

It was about the hottest night we could remember. Descending the mountain was to go from a tropic plateau to Dante's Inferno.

We passed filigree reflections. We turned onto the tar road leading to Rockingham Hospital. The world sweated, and the admitting driveway shone purplish, like a dog's tongue.

"This is a new building," said the nurse, mopping her face. "They saved by having no air conditioning."

I hung around, trying to cool Phyllis on her bed with a *Life* magazine fan. At last she kicked me out.

"It may be hours," she said. "Pete shouldn't be alone with the kids."

In the morning I called the maternity ward.

"Your wife's fine. The baby's fine," said the nurse.

"What is it?"

"A boy—real cute."

I got back before breakfast. Phyllis's cheeks were red and damp, but she beamed at the little papoose snuggled in her arm.

"Beth turned out to be Tim," she said. "Timothy Alan Morrill."

"His brothers will cheer."

Later I brought wild flowers from the mountain. Phyllis was sitting up, washed and combed.

She said, "Something funny dawned on me. All our boys are named after saints—Peter, Michael, Christopher, and Timothy. How did that happen?"

"Quite in the norm," I said, "I'm of the elect, too—Saint George."

She lifted her eyes to the ceiling. "Please excuse the blasphemy, Lord," she said.

So now we were six. Pete and Mike ranged around the mountain, new hunting knives flapping at their belts. (They swore they'd be careful with the big blades, and we decided a cut finger was probably the unavoidable price of self-reliance.) Chris, humming, wandered after crickets. Tim snoozed and howled in his crib.

"A few more animals and kids up here," said Phyllis, "and we can open our own Bronx Zoo."

Our roots are growing stronger, I thought. *Is there any sane reason why I should ever feel in the dumps again?*

I was still skirmishing with the blues. The new baby had brought a wave of happiness. But now and then the Black Dog (as Winston Churchill labeled depression) came slinking back, and I cursed myself for falling under its spell.

Then a curious thing happened, and I shook off the Black Dog forever.

It was a simple incident, really. I was making a

casual stop at the Bellows Falls railroad station. I stepped into the crumbling building to pick up a crate for Readex. The interior was dark and dismal, but at one end a light glowed.

I walked through a glass door into a small restaurant—and stopped, astonished. The place shone. Floor and walls were scrubbed. Magazines stood in neat racks. Behind a gleaming counter, a small woman cooked at a clean stove, and sweet odors floated up to the ceiling.

I parked on a stool beside men in overalls. I ordered coffee, and as the woman turned, I saw that she was partly paralyzed. The right side of her face looked frozen, and her right arm didn't work easily.

The coffee was fresh and aromatic. I sipped it, watching the woman limp about her duties: washing a dish, rubbing the counter. . . .

Here she was in a decaying station in a rural backwater, handicapped, alone—and doing her work as if it were the most important job in the world.

A heroine. Watching her ring up my five cents with her good hand, I thought: *If this woman has accepted her life so gracefully, what have I been bellyaching about?*

I walked outside and looked back. She was arranging some flowers in a cup on the counter.

"Courage," Ernest Hemingway said, "is grace under pressure."

In the following months this woman's example stuck with me. *Accept, accept.* This simplest of incidents pushed my mind back on the tracks. I turned to my tasks. I moved more slowly. I started noticing beauty again—a pearly birch, a lilac storm cloud.

With care, I inked some words on a 3-by-5-inch card and thumbtacked them over my desk: "Action is Character."—F. Scott Fitzgerald.

Each morning at 5:00 I glanced at them. They

meant, in my view, that a person's character was built by what he did. He could grow and change.

I wrote down other snips too: "Let us crown ourselves with rosebuds before they be withered" and "A man without mirth is a wagon without springs—every pebble makes a jolt."

Piece by piece I put together a working script for my life on Hartley Hill. I eased off on the night-construction hours. I developed a budget of sorts.

"This morning you whistled 'Sweet Georgia Brown,'" said Phyllis. "I haven't heard you whistle in an age."

"I've been away."

"Mmmmmmmmmmm."

"I think I skated close to a crack-up."

"You've been working too hard."

"So have you."

We carried groceries from the jeep. The field, mowed a few hours before, was aquiver with broken stalks and torn clover. The sky was red. The first cool of sundown, mixing with the heat of earth, made a propulsion of sweet smells.

At the door Phyllis stopped. "It's a good life up here, Zeke—and getting better."

"We didn't know a hell of a lot when we started."

"No—but how lucky we started!"

Well—yes. Build while you have the strength and capacity to dream. Pit yourself against hardship while you have a merciful lack of the overknowledge that cripples initiative.

"Think we're any smarter now, Marthy?"

She peered through the carrot greens sticking from the grocery bag.

"No dumber, anyhow. We made it, didn't we?"

She nodded at the Flat. Pete and Mike were setting up a tent. Chris was running back and forth handing

202

them stakes from a pile. In a minute, they would all be in high school. In another minute, they would be grown and gone.

"We'll be forty in just four years," she said.

"I don't give a hoot, do you?"

"No."

Where had our pioneer seasons gone? And who was this middle-aging couple reflected back at us in the front-door window—a lean man with crow's-feet around the eyes, a shapely woman holding some groceries?

"Whah," said a voice from inside the house.

"Oops, there goes the baby," said Phyllis. "Open the door, Zeke."

Epilogue

"One day in the country
Is worth a month in town."
— Christina Rossetti

TWENTY YEARS have passed. An editor's job offering irresistable benefits (a chance to work with top-drawer word-smiths, earn an English degree, and write a novel) has lured me from the mountain. But we still own the property. And we live only three hours away. Each summer we arrive with dog, cats, and tools—and a new project to gnaw on. We have planted flowers and nailed up birdhouses. We have cleared forest, built a road. . . .

Sometimes Phyllis and I sprawl in lawn chairs and watch whipped-cream clouds tumble down from Canada.

She'll say, "Remember when you raked the fireplace for nails?"

And I'll say, "Remember how you glued inner tubes to our worn-out shoe soles?"

Everything has changed. But it has been a steady flow of Time—very countryish—not a jet explosion. Richard Bradley and Roland Aldrich are gone, back into the earth they revered. Richard's big barn is down, replaced by a chalet.

204

Our boys are grown—Pete, the Vietnam vet; Mike, the M.A. student in sculpture; Chris, the college undergraduate; Tim, the tender Beth-to-have-been, who turned out to be an All-Conference High School quarterback. When they come back to the mountain, we have the muscle power to try anything. One summer we cut down a huge pine in Chester, hand-hewed it into a 12-foot beam, floated it across a pond, and hauled it to the Flat. Swaddled in canvas, it awaits installation as the Largest Mantel in Southern Vermont (which will have to wait for construction of our third fireplace, which will have to wait for a new room).

Readex has flourished, expanding along Main Street, Chester—a triumph of the Boni will.

In Saxtons River, the Old South Meeting House has come down, its Revere bell flown who knows where.

The Federated Church has finally moved full-time into the Baptist building. The old Congregational structure now houses the Historical Society, and you can find everything there from ancient village water pipe carved out of soap-stone to antique tools used in a vanished tinware industry.

The stretch has known tragedy, too. Gentle Ernie Dow, the raspberry man, put a gun to his head, and his wife died of cancer. The handsome son of our grocer was killed in a car wreck. The Benwares lost a young girl to a brain tumor.

But the march of the years has left our mountain a refuge for man and wildlife still. We wake to the flutings of song-birds. And the crystal air cleanses urban grit from our lungs. There may be more people around, but the area remains remote enough for a prudent person to wear something bright red in hunting season. (I once saw an out-of-state nimrod take dead aim at a brindle cow half-hidden in the brush; and a stray bullet once hit our back door.)

"We hung in up there, and it was worth it," said Phyllis. "We hacked it."

A while back, somebody got the bright idea of building an extension onto the living room.

"We can dig down and make a decent foundation from scratch," said Mike. "None of this Mickey Mouse, shim-and-cement jazz."

"Hold on there," I said. "Not one splinter of this building shakes."

"That's because the house is holding its breath."

We got picks and shovels. But ten inches deep, our tools chimed against stone. The whole area was ledge.

"If we want a room down there," I said, "we'll have to blast."

Silence. "Look out. The Old-Man's talking dynamite."

A neighbor, Al Hutchins, listened to our problem. "You need George Wood," he said.

George came, a Vermonter in overalls and battered sneakers. Pushing seventy, he had a grin like a little boy. He peered under the house.

"We can lay a charge in here and blow your living room sky-high," he said.

That, I said, would be interesting.

"Hell, I blew off the whole top of a mountain for the State Highway Department."

He backed his compressor around. We helped connect up the air hose and jackhammer. George drilled holes, starting twenty-five feet from the kitchen and working toward the house.

I said, "I got some plywood to cover the windows."

George looked surprised. "No need. Hell, those windows won't walk anyplace."

He dropped in the dynamite. He poked down plugs of sand with a broomstick. We lugged about thirty

206

old tires from his pickup, and he positioned them on top of the charge. He overlapped the tires in a careful way.

"Looks like a pile of doughnuts, don't it?" he said.

I remarked that there seemed to be a lot of holes for the explosion to come through.

"Well—to be safe, get the Missus out and say goodbye to the house."

We stood in the distance. George pushed the plunger.

KA-WHOOOM.

Tires and smoke mushroomed. Stones tore through the trees. But when we walked back, not a window was cracked.

"How'd you do that, George?"

"Damned if I know. Dumb luck."

We drilled and blasted for two days. It was quickly evident that George knew everything about blasting. In fact, he was a brilliant, self-taught engineer and geologist. He showed me parts of the ledge that were soft, parts that were dense, and parts that were grained so that they would crack in such-and-such a direction.

"Lot to know in this business, George."

"Oh, I ain't afraid of hard work," he said. "I've fought it successfully for years."

Hour by hour he chuckled and joked. He told stories of great explosions, nodding his grease-stained cap, twisting dynamite wires together while I looked on nervously. As our excavation moved closer to the house, he began to register alarm.

"Get the Missus out—and all dogs, cats, and mice. I just hope the rafters don't hit Saxtons River."

KA-WHOOOM.

I ran back, looking through the smoke. "No luck, George; you didn't get a window."

George made his hands quiver. "Why, I'm shaking so much I don't need no compressed air for the hammer—I'll just jiggle the bitch down."

Under the living room, he cut dynamite sticks in quarters and eighths. The explosions chewed at the ledge. Bite by bite the cellar hole widened, and upstairs not so much as an ashtray moved.

"Can't understand it," he said. "I expected we'd be on the moon by now."

As he drove out, compressor bouncing behind his pickup, the boys shook their heads. "There goes a cool hoss."

We slaved with crowbars and sledgehammers, taking out rock. We leveled the chunks along the breezeway and covered them with traprock, making a patio-porch that would heave flexibly with the frost.

Concrete blocks arrived, and we started building. Two guys mixed cement with hoes; three wielded trowels. Out came my collection of junk for reinforcing window lintels and corners—old pipe, carriage bolts, wire.

"Someday an archaeologist is going to take an X-ray of this plantation," said Phyllis. "He'll find all recorded history in the walls and chimneys."

We reached the upper floor level and went to Benware's Mill for 2-by-10-inch joists. The Benware boys were running the rig, peeling boards from the screaming blade and tossing them into a pile. Norman, seated on a pile of slabs with a can of beer, watched the logs roll down *thump-bang* and the clamps lock *click-snap*. The big blade sang. The diesel thundered. Sawdust flew.

"Cut you some two-by-tens right now, George."

I have never grown tired of watching expert sawyers make lumber. I took Norman's offered beer and sat down. My eye followed the bark-coated wood as it traveled down the rail, met the blade, and emerged as squared-off timber. The sweet tang of hemlock crinkled my nostrils.

Suddenly Norman stood up and turned off the engine. "Goddammit," he said softly, "you're going too fast."

Instantly the mill was full of shouting. Boys and father pointed and pounded fists and spread hands. But the engine stayed off.

"They git going too hefty sometimes," Norman explained, "and it ain't safe." He held up the stump of a thumb. "I ain't going to have this happen here."

After a while Norman allowed the mill to start again. The boys rolled the logs into position somewhat more slowly. I paid for my two-by-tens and left with a new respect for my neighbor.

We nailed on a plywood floor. I priced a circular steel stairway, from cellar to top, at $300. *Hah.* We built a stairs-and-landing affair out of scrap lumber at a cost of $6 for nails and screws.

In the end, we had a big deck of raised, waterproofed two-by-fours, surrounded by a sturdy two-by-six railing. And below, a room and part-cellar of concrete blocks. For the first time our cabin felt truly permanent, notched into the mountain like a fort.

As a finisher, we knocked a hole in the wall beside the living room fireplace and installed French doors. Phyllis stepped from the kitchen onto a sun-spanked area that overlooked miles of valley. Oak branches nodded above her head.

"Queen of the Sticks enters the Tuileries Gardens," I said.

She reclined on a chaise longue. "This is my style— and it only took a quarter of a century to get it."

"We wanted no unseemly haste."

I ran a wire to an electric outlet on the railing and built a coffee stand out of two-by-four remnants. We installed table and chairs. Overnight, the deck became the meeting and eating place for everyone.

On an evening not long ago Phyllis and I sat there. The sky was crumbling. Crimson cloud-wreckage glowed between the western trees, and a black hawk circled overhead. For some reason, memories floated down. Old songs seemed to drift through the air—*I don't want to walk without you, Bay-beee....*

"Remember those little drawings you sent me from your ship?" said Phyllis. "Cabin blissfully floating in flowers."

"Sun shining."

"Couple of horses out front."

Our eyes met, squinting. "*We* turned out to be the horses," I said.

We talked about high points and low points, weeks of delight and weeks of misery.

Phyllis said, "My all-time low was the day Chris ran out of the kitchen with the new soda straws I'd bought, saying, 'We're having a milk fight in the kitchen.' The washing machine had just quit."

My deepest ebb? I recalled a sloshy March afternoon when I stumbled into a Chester diner, my pocket heavy with three rejection slips.

"Nice day for kicking dogs and kids," somebody said, staring at the rain.

There was a wedding party jammed into two booths. In their wet Sunday suits, they looked as if they had been stuffed by taxidermists. All were eating soup. Not just slurping and gargling it—yodeling it.

I reached into my pocket and found no money. I walked out without my coffee.

"The scene got to me," I said. "Vermont Gothic—with music."

"Mr. Funds Unlimited meets his Romantic Dream," said Phyllis.

But there had been high points galore, too. As a matter of fact, right after leaving the diner, I had driven to Hartley Hill and found the rain changed to snow. Si Finch and a Bradley grandchild were on Big Baldy's slope, using a hunk of sheet-metal roofing as a sled.

"Yeoooooowwww!" they hollered. Their crazy sled shot down in a cloud of white, yawing and spinning. They looked wild and happy and their faces glowed.

"By the time I got to the cabin, I was up on my manic wave again," I said. "This was our country for sure."

"I never knew about that one, Zeke."

She said one of her best moments had come at a curious time. We had been through a threadbare winter. We had learned the primary law of finance: *If you're not close with a buck in the Vermont outback, you won't last long.* But somehow we had gotten a new rug and Phyllis had covered the sofa with bright brown-and-gold material. The pine walls had been waxed.

"The church ladies came," she said, "and you lighted a fire. I served tea. Everything was beautiful. When it came time for our donation to the Children's Fund, I took out our checkbook and said, 'This will be very modest.' I wrote a check for two dollars—in our first checkbook. They were satisfied. And I was proud."

"Very high-tone," I said.

"It *was*. I was proud of my house and my family."

So it has gone—and continues to go. Our Vermont venture began in romance, ripened in reality, and floats on in measured enthusiasm. Reading what young people are doing today, I have to admit that our effort doesn't seem so much. I showed Phyllis a

211

National Geographic piece about rugged kids pioneering in Alaska, another about a teen-ager sailing around the world alone.

"Our little caper is pretty tame beside these," I said.

She shrugged. "We all learned at the same knee—Mother Adversity."

When Phyllis and I started, my most recent job had grossed $2,850 for the year. We drove a hoary Buick with 1-candlepower headlights and Erector-set brakes. (We practically had to wrap our right foot around the axle to stop.) In previous summers we had lived in Army-surplus tents on a friend's property—and we didn't know beans about such things as faucet valves, masonry cement, and plywood.

But, flung willy-nilly into these problems, we learned. We found that ordinary people with little experience can quickly absorb the know-how of carpenters, masons, and electricians—and that these craftsmen are eager to teach, if properly approached. We found that you can work harder than you think you can, that you can condition yourself to ignore vexations which seem mountainous.

I suppose our Vermont property was always in danger of slipping out of our lubberly hands. We were naïve about the drains of mortgage, insurance, and taxes. We knew nothing about the impact of isolation on ordinarily gregarious people.

However, once our talons were dug in, there was nothing to do but hang on. Whence could we flee? The problem of tonight's warmth and tomorrow's food always loomed, and it kept us in motion. We lost track of exact dates. Our cycles were pegged to seasonal mileposts—the gold-dappling of the hills or when the brook ice broke.

So it's not all that bad to fall under the yoke of

necessity for a while. It sharpens your survival instincts.

Recently I stood on the Knoll in soft twilight. A warm wind was blowing rather strongly, and the knee-high grass nodded. Silky pollen whipped past.

In the valley, the fireflies were out. Thousands of these little lights winked in the fields, and they looked like the rifle flashes of a Civil War battle.

Suddenly I heard cries. Three children scampered along the edge of the pond. Their hair blew and their bare feet twinkled. They kicked the water. They snatched up leaves and flung them.

They came to our telephone pole. They looked up. They put their ears to the pole, listening to the hum of the wires. ("What a recipe for preserving wood, perchance, to keep it from rotting," said Thoreau of wired telegraph posts, "to fill its pores with music!")

These scampering kids were Richard Bradley's great-grandchildren.

Now, that's *continuity*. And there seems to be a growing amount of it on Hartley Hill these days. The rusty pickups rattle by, loaded with cows or kids. Chain saws whine in the woods. Across from the Dows', two log cabins are rising, built from scratch by a pair of shaggy-haired youths.

Best of all, a young couple have bought the old Bradley farmhouse, and they give every indication of sticking it out up here.

"Their name's Kennedy," said Phyllis, as we drove by one October afternoon. "They have a little boy—just like Pete was."

"They have an old car, too—just the way we did," I said.

The Kennedys were out on their lawn, unloading wood from a truck. They moved amid piles of fresh-dug earth, concrete blocks, bricks, and timbers. You could tell they were midstream in rebuilding the foundation, girding themselves for the winter.

The girl waved. The young husband nodded. The small son pointed a stick at us.

"Lucky," said Phyllis softly.